A Tribute to
Amatu'l-Bahá Rúḥíyyih Khánum

A
TRIBUTE
TO
AMATU'L-BAHÁ RÚḤÍYYIH KHÁNUM

by
Violette Nakhjavani

Printed in Canada

ISBN 0-88867-105-9

A joint project of

Bahá'í Canada
Publications

7200 Leslie Street
Thornhill, Ontario
Canada L3T 6L8

Nine Pines Publishing
26 Concourse Gate
Nepean, Ontario
Canada K2E 7T7

Contents

List of Illustrations

Acknowledgements

The writing of this tribute in its present form would not have been possible without the indispensable assistance of Nell Golden, the trusted and much-loved secretary of Amatu'l-Bahá, whose meticulous research into the body of documents about Rúḥíyyih Khánum's life provided many of the facts incorporated into this text which she also most kindly and painstakingly typeset. I also wish to express my appreciation and deep gratitude to my daughter Bahiyyih Nakhjavani for her invaluable help in editing this manuscript and to Audrey Marcus for designing the cover.

⌘

Note: Material in the tribute has been taken from the private papers of Amatu'l-Bahá Rúḥíyyih Khánum. Unfortunately so far the original letter of May Maxwell to Agnes Alexander quoted on pages 4–6 has not been found but the text of the letter suggests a great deal of credibility as it is in agreement in its essentials with the diary notes found among the papers of Mírzá 'Alí Akbar Nakhjavání.

Prologue

On January 19th in the year 2000, a lady passed away from this world. She was unique, and with her passing a chapter ended, a page of history turned. And when Amatu'l-Bahá Rúḥíyyih Khánum's earthly remains were buried a few days later, the Universal House of Justice laid her to rest in a place that is also unique. For her grave is not on the mountainside among the sacred monuments of the Greatest Holy Leaf and other members of the family of Bahá'u'lláh nor is it in the cemetery where Bahá'ís at the World Centre have been buried for so many decades past. But like her place in history, it seems, almost, to have been prepared for her by Shoghi Effendi, and lies in a garden all on its own. Flanked on each side by associations with those who dominated her life—her mother May Maxwell and her own Guardian—her grave is in the little park opposite the Master's House where she lived for 63 years and in which she left her own unique mark.

Although her place in history has thus been symbolically fixed at her death, it will be much more difficult to frame and define a life as rich and varied as that of Mary Maxwell, who was later given the name and title of Amatu'l-Bahá Rúḥíyyih Khánum by her beloved husband and her Guardian. We are still too close to her to be able to understand the true value of her services to the Bahá'í world community and still too limited in our grasp of our own history to be able to evaluate the different perspectives afforded by her personality. Perhaps we are also still too influenced at the present time by the twin tendencies to over-exaggerate and underestimate in the writing of biography, to be able to do her justice. For we have not yet learned to distinguish between proper objectivity and voyeurism, between tiresome hagiography and the telling of a person's spiritual story. Perhaps it is too soon to write about the life of Rúḥíyyih Kh̲ánum.

Certainly, I am no writer and would never presume to call myself the biographer of someone as dynamic and forceful as 'Amatu'l-Bahá. But owing to the immense honour I have had during these past forty years, of knowing her and hearing the ways in which she chose to define and to describe herself, I feel a certain responsibility to make some first, poor and inadequate attempt to summarize the broad outlines of her life.

The following monograph, in three parts, is a summary of her story within a simple chronological framework of events. These three parts, from Mary Maxwell's birth to Rúḥíyyih Kh̲ánum's final years, cover her early years, her years of marriage to Shoghi Effendi, and her final years of service and travels. Like the perspectives that flank her resting-place, they also describe the broad influences of her life: on one side, the Old Pilgrim House, where the very room in which her mother stayed now overlooks her grave; on the other, the dining room of No.10 Haparsim, in which she sat by the Guardian's side for all the years of her marriage; and opposite, the House of 'Abdu'l-Bahá, a house redolent with history, marked by suffering and death, a house she filled with life and laughter and to which those whom she had met in the four corners of the world came and enjoyed her hospitality.

It is a multi-faceted story with these and many more dimensions. No doubt others more qualified than myself will explore it further and will in the future understand it better than I can today. But despite its modesty and insufficiency, I would like to offer this small tribute to her, with my love.

VIOLETTE NAKHJAVANI

Haifa, Israel
August 2000, in memory
of Amatu'l-Bahá's 90th birthday

I

Early Years

I

The birth of Mary Sutherland Maxwell, on August 8th, in the Hahnemann Hospital, later known as The Fifth Avenue Hospital, in New York City, was the hottest news to hit the North American Bahá'í community in the summer of 1910. Ever since May Bolles had accepted the Faith of Bahá'u'lláh, she had been known and loved by all the early Bahá'ís as one of the foremost disciples of 'Abdu'l-Bahá; her husband, Sutherland Maxwell, was a distinguished architect in Canada and their home in Montreal a place of culture and spiritual vitality. When the Bahá'ís read the announcement: "A little daughter has come to bless the home of Mr. and Mrs. W. S. Maxwell of Montreal, Canada", in Vol. 1, issue 9 of the *Star of the West* on August 20th, it must have caused many flutters of excited interest amongst them. There must have been many who expressed their congratulations and sent their good wishes.

> *In the garden of existence a rose hath bloomed with the utmost freshness, fragrance and beauty. Educate her according to the divine teachings so that she may grow up to be a real Bahá'í and strive with all thy heart, that she may receive the Holy Spirit.*

These words of the Centre of the Covenant, 'Abdu'l-Bahá, in a Tablet dated March 2, 1911, were addressed to May Maxwell when Mary was just seven months old and were surely the greatest confirmation she had ever received of this blessing. The circumstances of her little girl's birth were like a fairy tale and have been repeated, and frequently distorted, since they were recorded in the early years of this century. May Maxwell gives us the original version in a letter she wrote to Agnes Alexander, on May 7, 1910:

My Dearest Agnes,

All of your dear letters have been received and . . . You must have wondered that I could remain so silent in spite of all your love and kindness but you will understand when I tell you that this winter has been one of great physical weakness and suffering for me, so that I have been most of the time unable to write, or to make any effort.

A little more than a year ago when I was in Acca I was passing one evening in the twilight in front of the Master's door. His daughter Rouha was with me and in my arms I held her wee babe. I suddenly saw Our Beloved Lord framed in the doorway gazing attentively upon me—then He said—"You love that baby?"

"Oh! I love him," I replied—and after a pause Our Lord said: "Come here, come in here," and I stood before Him in His room, with the baby in my arms and Rouha by my side. Then the Blessed one sat looking at us; and He said to me: "Would you like to have a baby?" and I answered, "I should be so happy to have one—" and He said, "Do you know why you never had one? It is because you were a chosen maidservant of God—you were called for the service of God—you could not have children because you had to devote your time to the service of the Cause. This is the only reason; this is the only reason."

I stood with bowed head before Him and after a little silence He said, "Speak, do you choose to have a child, you may choose!"

Then I looked at Him with all my heart and soul and adoration, and I said, "I choose whatever God chooses—I have no choice but His." Although those words were very simple—in them I renounced all hope of Motherhood. Then 'Abdu'l-Bahá arose quickly and came to me and clasped me in His arms with the greatest love and joy, and He said: "That is the best choice, the Will of God is the best choice", and walking up and down the room He continued, "I will pray for you, that God will send you that which is best for you. Be sure of this, that God will send you that which is best for you—" and this He repeated several times.

Thus ended this never-to-be forgotten scene—but I cannot describe its reality—the deep significance of those moments—the atmosphere of beauty and sanctity which pervaded the little room—the surrender of a soul in the Presence of the Lord—the quiet twilight on earth mingling with the effulgent purity and peace of the Kingdom of God.

And regarding the Adored One Himself—what can we say? Such love—such wondrous love—revealed in Face and Voice and Eyes and Touch! A love so tender to understand, so strong to redeem! He desired for me as for all, the highest and best—not the wayward mortal desiring—not even the natural human longings—not even the pure flower of Motherhood—but the surrender of the soul to God by which alone it attains the apex of severance and sanctity, and becomes enkindled with the Fire of Eternal Love.

And so I have told you, my Agnes—of one scene of those divine and perfect days in the Kingdom of God—and in time I shall hope to tell you all . . . For those days live forever, far above the world—and I long to have you and all the dear ones share their sacred fruits. And now my lamb I am going to confide to you a secret which is the sequel to what I have told you. Our dear Lord has favored His maidservant past all her hope, and by the pure showers of His Bounty has watered the seed of life, and is bringing forth a child. In a few months Inchallah, the babe He is sending to my husband and me will be born, and I beg for your prayers, both for the little one and for myself—for I am not strong—nor young! and physically I am passing through some trials—and this winter I had a

> fall which nearly proved fatal. I have not told the friends—even the most intimate—but I wanted you to know—and I know you will keep my confidence.

May took her Lord's injunctions to heart. She strove to educate her precious, God-given daughter according to the divine teachings just as He had instructed her to do. She did her utmost to ensure that her little Mary should grow up "to be a real Bahá'í" in order that she might indeed be able to "receive the Holy Spirit" just as the Master promised.

Some years ago, Amatu'l-Bahá showed me a small black photo album which she had found in the desk drawer of the beloved Guardian after his passing. He had arranged his favourite photographs of Mary Maxwell in this album, from babyhood through to her teenage years. And there was among them a photograph of her at age five of which he was particularly fond. In a little note written by May Maxwell herself we find a description very similar to this photograph, which warms the heart. She writes:

> Mary was just five years old when this picture of her bursting thru the daisy beds was taken. This picture reveals almost all of Mary. If we were so developed that we could see the inner things as well as the outer we would know all about Mary by studying this picture. Here she is in her own world—the kingdom of Nature which she so loves—the sun, the air, the flowers, everything that grows is dear and familiar to her. Most of all the animal world from the tiniest bug to the king of the animal kingdom Mary adores—and this lion king is the favourite of all. Ever since she was a toddling baby Mother Nature has held sway over the passionate love of this child—so that in the even brief years of her life she has learned all about beetles, worms, caterpillars, flies, ants, bees, wasps, hornets, spiders, etc.—where they live, how they live, what they eat, and what changes

> they undergo. She knows about toads, frogs, lizards, snakes, mud eels, and I don't know what slimy creatures. All this knowledge she has gained at first hand, straight from the source by watching these creatures—catching them—keeping them for a time and feeding them—and then making people read her all about them in books.

Rúḥíyyih Khánum used to refer to her formal education as "patchy", recalling her school days to have been few and far between. The traditional educational methods of the time tended to be rigid and authoritarian, narrow-minded and dictatorial, and little Mary may have suffered from these methods, for her spirit was untrammelled and her will strong. Her mother's concern to provide her with the "freedom" which 'Abdu'l-Bahá had prescribed is reflected in a letter addressed to Marion Holley (Hofman) dated July 15th, 1937, in which May Maxwell tells about Mary's early training:

> . . . You may know that when Rúḥíyyih was three or four years old I imported the first set (Montessori Method) to Canada, with a Montessori teacher from New York and established the first school of this type in Canada (Montreal) in our own home. . . . It really did wonders for her and the other eight children, and 'Abdu'l-Bahá, with whom I discussed Montessori's work in 1912, said that she was the greatest modern psychologist . . . It was through all this that I became interested in the "Movement of Progress and Education" of which I was practically a charter member and subscribed to their magazine edited by Stanwood Cobb.

After such beginnings, she also had a year of schooling in Montreal, a few months in Chevy Chase Country Day School in Maryland and another year in Weston High School in Montreal. Between these haphazard school experiences she was tutored at home by governesses and private teachers, but this was the sum total of her scholastic training until she later became a part-time student at McGill University, where she used to say she invariably arrived at her 9.00 A.M. class late! Her mother, who suffered from nervous disorders and insomnia throughout her life, could not bear to wake Mary up early in the mornings as she had a theory that young people's sleep should never be disturbed! Be that as it may, there is a copy of her paper, dated May 1931, for the Department of Economics at McGill University entitled "The Bahá'í System of Public Finance" by Mary Maxwell, on which she herself has written: "I passed with 2nd class honours on this in a fourth year course!" Rúḥíyyih Khánum used to explain that the reason for her unconventional upbringing and education was her mother's bad health, and the constant fear she had of losing her. When she was away from home, she would become acutely anxious for her mother, who was physically fragile and had come close to death on many occasions.

Yet despite these inconsistencies of education, she was to become a well-read and knowledgeable person, with a consuming interest in a variety of subjects. Her thirst for acquiring knowledge was insatiable and throughout her life, practically to the very end, she clipped articles from the daily papers which caught her attention because they reflected Bahá'í themes or subjects of particular interest to her. She loved to have her favourite fairy tales read to her when she was young, and since she did not want to leave a story unfinished when her mother put her to bed, she simply learned to read unaided in order to go on reading the story to the end. It may have been this habit which accustomed her to reading late at night. She used to say, "I have been weaned on the classical European fairy tales of the Brothers Grimm and Hans Christian Andersen."

The proud and happy May Maxwell with her baby Mary;
one of the earliest photographs of Mary, circa 1910

Mary Maxwell, about two years old, the age when she first met 'Abdu'l-Bahá, circa 1912

Age four – all dressed up! Circa 1914

"Mary was just five years old when this picture of her bursting through the daisy beds was taken", wrote May Maxwell

The girls who were called to unveil the Tablets of the Divine Plan. Mary (centre), nearly nine years old, was one of the two girls to unveil the Tablets revealed for Canada. New York, April 26–30, 1919

Mary Maxwell, at the time of her first pilgrimage,
circa 1923

The Oz books were also among her favourites. These beautiful editions, some of which were graced with original drawings by Arthur Rackham and Kay Neilson, were treasured by her to the very end of her life. Her beloved father, from whom she inherited her artistic abilities, her knowledge of antiques, and her love of good books, increased this collection whenever he came across a particularly beautiful edition of her favourites.

She had a full, free and happy childhood. Her only sorrows at this time, which she would speak of until late in life, were the periods of separation from her beloved mother. May Maxwell was a devoted and dedicated servant of the Cause, a member of several Bahá'í administrative bodies, as well as one of the star teachers of the Faith. She suffered greatly from the extreme cold of Montreal and her ill health would often keep her away from her home for two or more months at a time. She would go to New York or Wilmette to attend meetings, would become ill and then could not return home for several weeks. The physical attachment and spiritual kinship that connected mother and daughter was singular and strong. Rúḥíyyih Khánum often said, "If Bahá'ís believed in such things as 'soul mates', my mother and I would be like that." This bond, consciously nurtured by May Maxwell herself, is beautifully expressed in a letter written by the mother to her daughter some years later:

> . . . however often I have been compelled to leave you since you were a little child, for the sake of this great Cause in which we are united, and however lonely you may have often been, you never suffered alone, because I was always with you, I felt for you more deeply than you can ever realize, and it is out of the pangs of this mighty motherlove that my spiritual motherhood to you has been born.

However arbitrary and independent may have been her formal intellectual education, there are clear indications that her spiritual training was pursued with rigour and unrelenting discipline. It was a training whose hallmark was love and whose main characteristic was obedience to the Covenant. There is a vast amount of correspondence between May Maxwell and 'Abdu'l-Bahá in which references can be found to the little girl, many of which indicate the attention and love of the Master for the child. In a rare letter from Mr. W. S. Maxwell to 'Abdu'l-Bahá, dated March 12th, 1915, he says, "Little Mary is a joy to us and thinks of you very frequently. She loves you with a deep and true love and understanding." Her spiritual training had clearly begun from a very early age.

Rúḥíyyih Khánum was often asked if she remembered 'Abdu'l-Bahá's three-day visit to their home during the fall of 1912. She would answer with her characteristic honesty, "I was only two years old. I don't think I remember it, but all my life I heard my mother telling me in detail of all of those precious and blessed days, so the events imprinted on my subconscious seem like my own memories." May Maxwell recorded in her notes a particularly moving reference to the arrival of 'Abdu'l-Bahá in the Maxwell home on the night of August 30th, 1912, and His words on that occasion:

> ". . . home", He said, "all that is in it is mine"—turning with an ineffable look He continued—"You are mine—your husband and child. This is my home." He was cold and we lighted a fire. He looked about and He asked where the child was. When we said that she was sleeping He told us not to disturb her and added, "dark indeed is the home where there is no child."

There is an especially touching story about this visit,

told by 'Abdu'l-Bahá Himself to His companions and recorded in the memoirs of A. A. Nakhjavani. 'Abdu'l-Bahá told them:

> "Today I was resting on the *chaise longue* in my bedroom and the door opened. The little girl came in to me and pushed my eyelids up with her small finger and said, 'Wake up, 'Abdu'l-Bahá!' I took her in my arms and placed her head on my chest and we both had a good sleep."

When Rúḥíyyih Kh͟ánum repeated this story in later years she used to say that once when her mother complained to 'Abdu'l-Bahá that she was naughty, the Master had said, "Leave her alone. She is the essence of sweetness."

The years of 'Abdu'l-Bahá's ministry were drawing to a close with World War I, and as a precursor to His Will and Testament, He sent the Tablets of the Divine Plan to the Bahá'ís of the West. It was a sacred legacy to the North American continent and the Bahá'ís celebrated this epoch-making event with befitting solemnity. Nine young girls were chosen from the community, and, to the sound of solemn music, drew aside the curtains covering the original handwritten Tablets of 'Abdu'l-Bahá. Mary Maxwell, adorned in a new pink dress, and her best childhood friend, Elizabeth Coristine of Montreal, were privileged to unveil the first and second of these Tablets for Canada in a spectacular *tableau vivant* which took place in the Hotel McAlpin in New York on April 29th, 1919 at 10:00 a.m. It was shortly before Mary's ninth birthday and the end of the Heroic Age of the Faith of Bahá'u'lláh.

The passing of 'Abdu'l-Bahá, in November 1921, devastated the whole Bahá'í community, both in the East and West, but the blow proved almost fatal to May Maxwell, who was given the news abruptly and brutally, over the telephone, without any forewarning. She was so shattered and so shaken in body and soul that she may have become a permanent invalid had not Mr. Maxwell finally intervened. He convinced her that the only way she would be able to leave her wheelchair was if she went to visit the Shrines in the Holy Land and met her beloved Guardian, face to face. And he thought Mary should go with her. She used to say in later years, "My father was busy with his work at the Chateau Frontenac and my mother was an invalid. There was no one else to accompany her but me and an Irish Catholic maid. And I was twelve years old."

Just seventeen months after the Ascension of the Master and four months before her 13th birthday, therefore, they set sail from New York for the Holy Land, on April 29th, 1923. This was Mary's first pilgrimage and left an indelible impression and many memories in her heart and mind. In later years she recalled, in a personal letter, how she was touched by "the spirit of service" she discovered in Haifa:

> . . . a Queen or a beggar woman would be met with the same loving sweetness. Indeed it was this divine normality that really confirmed me here as a little girl of twelve years.

It was the first time she met the beloved Guardian and she often described that meeting with a sweet pleasure in the remembrance. They were installed in the Old Western Pilgrim House at the end of Persian Street and her mother, who had not been able to walk for over a year, was resting in bed. Since her nights were frequently sleepless and her nerves delicate, Mary had learned from an early age to protect her from intrusion and was vigilant against disturbances. She said that she was in the hallway of the Pilgrim House when the door suddenly opened and a young man stepped in, with a swift, deft movement, and asked if he could see Mrs. Maxwell. She was a tall girl for her age, fully grown and physically well-developed already. She said she pulled herself up to her full height and, looking him squarely in the eyes, asked to know, with considerable dignity and aplomb, who it was who wished to see Mrs. Maxwell. The young gentleman meekly replied, "I am Shoghi Effendi", upon which she turned tail and fled into her mother's room in mortified embarrassment. Hiding her head, as she used to say "like a puppy", beneath her mother's pillows, she could only point to the door and gasp, "He—he—is there!" when her mother asked her what the matter was. And when May Maxwell found out who it was behind the door, she said, "Pull yourself together, Mary, and go and invite him in."

They were away from Montreal for almost a year. Shoghi Effendi, before leaving for Europe that summer—for he was exhausted by the weight of his responsibilities and needed to recuperate his own strength—advised Mrs. Maxwell to spend the time in Egypt, and so during his absence from the Middle East she stayed in Port Said with her daughter and her maid. After his return, Shoghi Effendi recalled them to Haifa for another lengthy stay, as a result of which they had two pilgrimages during that single year. May came back to the States in 1924, in time to attend the National Bahá'í Convention. Filled with joy and restored to health, she redoubled her efforts in the teaching work and began to educate the friends in the Bahá'í Administration, in which she had been carefully instructed by Shoghi Effendi during her pilgrimage.

Two years later, Mary accompanied Juliet Thompson and Daisy Smythe to the Holy Land. They were two of her mother's closest friends, and Juliet Thompson, too, had been designated by the Master as His "disciple". On this pilgrimage Mary often spoke of her deep sorrow at leaving the Greatest Holy Leaf, whose high station she had come to recognize and cherish despite her own youth, and whom she loved dearly despite the difference of their ages. During her first pilgrimage, the Greatest Holy Leaf had asked to see Mary's performance of the Egyptian 'shimmy', which she had learned that summer in Port Said, and had laughed till the tears rolled down her cheeks when young Mary, dressed in full costume, with *kohl* around her eyes and a drum under her arm, had sung and danced before her in the Master's House. Now on this second pilgrimage it was a more mature Mary who understood with sadness that this would be the last time she would see Bahíyyih Khánum, the greatest lady and heroine of the Bahá'í Dispensation, whom she described as the essence of meekness and gentleness.

Back in Canada, she threw herself eagerly into all kinds of youth activities, both within the Bahá'í administration as well as elsewhere, all of which were just as important to her as the studies she pursued with equal enthusiasm. From then on she was continuously involved in membership on committees and in her efforts to promote the cause of racial amity. Shortly before she was 16, she became a member of the Executive Committee of The Fellowship of Canadian Youth for Peace, serving as its Treasurer. On November 30th, 1928, her mother wrote, "Mary is well and doing splendid work with her studies, besides the 'Fratority' Society whose membership is constantly extending and whose influence is becoming a strong power for inter-racial amity of all kinds in this city." As was expected, soon after she had turned 21, she was elected on the Local Spiritual Assembly of Montreal, as well as on the Teaching Committee.

Her training in oratory and public speaking too began early. She used to mention an incident which took place after her return from her second pilgrimage, when she was almost 16. In a Bahá'í meeting at Green Acre, one of the well-known old Bahá'ís paused in his lecture unexpectedly and, turning to young Mary Maxwell, asked her to come up on the platform and tell the friends about her experiences in the Holy Land. She said she was shocked and tried to escape through the door but was caught before she could get away. The speaker reminded her that since she had had the great privilege of visiting the Holy Shrines and hearing the beloved Guardian, it was her duty to share these bounties with others!

From informal talks like this she graduated to more formal engagements, which required conscious preparation, both of thought and spirit. Just before her nineteenth birthday, she spoke at the National Bahá'í Convention in a manner that evidently touched many peoples' hearts and minds. In a letter to May Maxwell after this event Elizabeth Herlitz writes, "Sorry I did not hear your daughter speak on Saturday eve during the Convention. I was told I had missed one of the outstanding features of the entire Bahá'í Program."

Increasingly, too, she began to accompany her mother on teaching trips, during which she had occasion not only to observe her mother's manner of giving Bahá'í talks but also to learn how to lecture herself, in the Bahá'í spirit. May writes: "Mary and I have been on a three weeks' teaching trip since the Convention. . . . I have been entirely submerged in the field of teaching with Mary where we have done our first united work together with remarkable results . . ." It was soon after this trip that she received her first letter from the beloved Guardian, dated May 29th and written in his own hand:

My dear co-worker:

I am much pleased to learn of your growing activities in the Cause & I will supplicate from the depths of my heart in your behalf at the holy Shrines that the Beloved may graciously guide you & assist you to render inestimable services to His Cause in the days to come.

Your true brother,

Shoghi

One of the most wonderful events of her life, at the age of 20, was a lecture she delivered in New York City at the Friends' Meeting House. Her subject, "Mysticism in the Bahá'í Religion", was daunting and all the other speakers at this Congress were seasoned lecturers and famous orators. One of these, Syud Hossain, was described as an "incomparable lecturer on the Orient, world peace and international relations", and was the editor of "The New Orient". Several well-known university professors, bishops and canons of different churches also addressed the Congress, and at the end of the programme, there was also to be a talk given by the conceited enemy of the Bahá'í Faith, Ahmad Sohrab. After her lecture she received a standing ovation, and on that same day was given the following cable: "HEARTY CONGRATULATIONS ON YOUR BEAUTIFUL CONSCIENTIOUS AND ABLE PRESENTATION OF A GREAT AND DIFFICULT THEME I AM HAPPY AND PROUD OF YOU—SYUD HOSSAIN".

Her writing began early too. She wrote books and plays and poetry, and her highest hope was to one day become an author. She busied herself with early literary efforts, writing articles with such titles as "Have the Emotions a Place Today?" She was developing that diversity and range of skills that would serve to make of her a perfect instrument of service in the hands of her beloved Guardian, who noted her progress with keen interest.

May and Mary Maxwell in Ramleh, Egypt, the time of Mary's first pilgrimage, 1923

Fifteen-year-old Mary Maxwell, circa 1925

Sixteen-year-old Mary Maxwell, the year of her second pilgrimage, 1926

The inner and outer beauty already in full evidence,
circa 1926

When a copy of the translation of Nabíl's Narrative by the beloved Guardian, *The Dawn-Breakers*, reached the Maxwells, they wrote a letter of gratitude to Shoghi Effendi, and in reply he encouraged Mary to study this book and lecture on it. The article she wrote entitled 'The Re-florescence of Historical Romance in Nabil', which he later included in *The Bahá'í World*, Volume V (1932–34), was surely a result of the Guardian's direct encouragement, and the ardent, youthful enthusiasm which it reveals must have informed her unforgettable lectures on the Heroic Age of the Cause. These were first given in Montreal and then later in Green Acre, continued in Louhelen, and finally at Esslingen in Germany.

A letter of Shoghi Effendi's to May Maxwell at this time shows how closely he was following the development and spiritual training of this remarkable young woman. It was as though he had undertaken her spiritual education himself, was guiding her choices and carefully directing her attentions so that she would not dissipate her spiritual potential:

> I feel that she should, while pursuing her studies, devote her energies to an intensive study of, & vigorous service to, the Cause, of which I hope & trust she will grow to become a brilliant and universally honoured exponent. I am sure, far from feeling disappointed or hurt at my suggestion, she will redouble in her activities & efforts to approach & attain the high standard destined for her by the beloved Master. Your plan of travelling with her throughout Canada in the service of the Cause is a splendid one & highly opportune. Kindly assure her & her dear father of my best wishes & prayers for their happiness welfare & success.
>
> Your true & affectionate brother,
>
> Shoghi

In May 1933, Mary spent several weeks in Washington,

D.C., first with her mother and then alone, teaching the Faith and concentrating her efforts on finding ways to draw the two opposing races together, for the cause of racial unity was close to her heart and the rights and responsibilities of both races was a subject that touched her keenly throughout her life. On November 20th of that year she spoke at the "coloured people's Church" in Montreal. Fred Schopflocher wrote to May about this event, saying,

> She had everybody spellbound and how that girl looked, just ravishing, just the daughter of her mother! With a pure white blouse she stood forth like the silvery moon in a dark, dark night and her little green hat, green in its symbol, a beacon of hope, faith and assurance. I truly was proud of the girl, my dear little Mary and you know, May, it is not often that I enthuse, there is conviction to the truth behind it. . . .
>
> Well this affair was wonderful. Mr. Este was at his best . . . and practically announced himself a Bahá'í from the pulpit and his congregation with it.

Rev. Este, the parson of this Church, remained a lifelong friend of Rúḥíyyih Khánum's, despite the fact that he never actually became a Bahá'í. In 1970, during my first visit to the Americas, I met him in Montreal, when he was elderly and retired. But despite his frailty he came especially to the Maxwell home, now the Shrine, to see Rúḥíyyih Khánum, and it was clear that a deep love and friendship had existed between them since that occasion in 1934.

In contrast to her earnest efforts at promoting Bahá'í principles at the grass roots, Mary attended official functions with her father at home in Montreal during her early twenties, meeting the Governor-General of Canada at events such as the Royal Canadian Academy's Fifty-

Fourth Exhibition. It was this balance between high and low, between her obligations to the Bahá'í community in particular and society at large that would serve her so well in later years. She always had the ability to mingle with officialdom and humble folk with equal ease; her support of local Bahá'í teaching work as well as social issues at the international level was equally enthusiastic throughout her life.

Rúḥíyyih Khánum used to say that as a young woman she had very much wanted to learn Spanish but when, in 1935, civil war threatened her plans to go to Spain for this purpose, she was induced to accompany her cousins Jeanne and Randolph Bolles to Germany instead. Her aunt, who was German herself, accompanied them and they sailed for Europe on July 10th. From August of that same year, May also joined them and, for the next year and a half, while May spent most of her time teaching and helping the friends in France and Belgium, Mary paralleled her mother's work in Germany.

She became so enamoured of Germany during this time that she asked Shoghi Effendi if she might stay in this country rather than returning to travel with her mother. May writes that Mary was "greatly encouraged by the Guardian to concentrate her efforts where her heart is!" She was, as her mother puts it, "Among a people who seem so akin to her that—as I believe I wrote you—her whole nature has undergone a radical change under this new and profound influence." An old-time Montreal friend, S. H. Abramson, visiting in Europe, writes to May that, "Mary has fallen in love with Germany and become almost 100% German." She learned the language with such fluency and spoke with so perfect an accent that many thought her to be German. She used to say when she travelled in northern Germany people would ask her if she was from the south, and when she was in the south, they thought she was from the north!

To have lived in Germany during its most critical period in the twentieth century, with her attention fixed solely on the work of the Cause, her efforts given entirely to the development of its institutions, and her time spent primarily in the company of Bahá'ís who were later destined to suffer so terribly under Hitler's régime, is surely an indication of the mettle she was made of. Tall and beautiful, under a crown of light brown hair and dressed in a 'dirndl', she passed through the fire unscathed as the jack boots marched and the banners thickened the air about her. How strong was her obedience to her Guardian during this period, and how much this obedience must have protected her at this fearful time. For she received encouragement every step of the way, and guidance. In addition, both she and her mother received a warm invitation to come to the Holy Land at the end of their extended stay in Europe. Shoghi Effendi's secretary writes to May Maxwell on January 21st, 1936 that:

> The Guardian is very much encouraged & gratified to learn of the progress & success of your dear daughter's activities in the teaching field. He wishes you to congratulate her most heartily upon the success that has attended her work in Munich. He hopes that her "first German offspring" Mr. Alfonse Giesel will, as a result of such a contact, become a most active & leading servant of the Cause in Germany.

In the postscript below, the Guardian writes, in his own hand:

> Dearly-beloved co-worker:
>
> I wish to assure you in person of a most hearty wel-

> come. Your distinguished services, so loyally, courageously & devotedly rendered, in both the European & American continents, fully entitle you to visit the Holy Shrines & to draw fresh inspiration from the Source of His inexhaustible grace. I am profoundly thankful for what you, Mary & Mrs. Bolles have achieved, & for the spirit which animates you in His service. The Beloved is well-pleased with the many evidences of your exemplary devotion to His Cause & of perseverance in the path of service. Affectionately
>
> Shoghi

A week later, the Guardian's secretary addressed a letter to Mary Maxwell herself, on behalf of Shoghi Effendi. His guidance must have seemed like a bright beacon before her in the midst of a darkening Europe, in which the spirit was being extinguished more and more:

> The Guardian is very pleased, indeed to learn that you are so much longing to visit the Holy Shrines, after so many years. He wishes me, therefore, to hasten in extending to you a most hearty welcome. Your dear Mother, who we have just learned is now in Paris, has also expressed a desire to visit Haifa, and the Guardian has extended to her too, a most cordial invitation.
>
> Before your coming to Haifa Shoghi Effendi would advise you to visit the centers in Germany and if possible to extend your trip to Austria and the Balkans where we have now a chain of active and prosperous communities that link the Western with the Eastern part of Europe. He would even suggest that you follow that route when you come to Haifa, as this would be of great interest to you, and of invaluable encouragement to the friends in these new and somewhat isolated centers.

Shoghi Effendi added, in his postscript:

> Dear and valued co-worker:

I wish to assure you in person of a hearty welcome to visit the Holy Land and lay your head on the sacred Threshold after having rendered valuable services in the Faith in both America and Europe. For those you have asked me to pray, in your letters, I will supplicate the blessings of Bahá'u'lláh. Rest assured. Your true brother,

Shoghi

Mary Maxwell fulfilled the injunctions of the beloved Guardian. She travelled to every single community in Germany, met every isolated believer, group, or Assembly, from north to south and east to west of the country. By the time she had accomplished this task, a year had passed and the rumblings of war were upon them in earnest. It was impossible now to travel through the Balkans or Austria, and she and her mother were then urged by Shoghi Effendi to come to the Holy Land directly. It was a turning point.

When mother and daughter registered their names in the Pilgrims' book in Haifa on January 12th, 1937, another chapter began in the life of Mary Maxwell. Her training and spiritual education were over. She had passed the test and come out true. As Shoghi Effendi told May Maxwell on this pilgrimage, her daughter now had the spiritual foundation on which she could be "moulded and disciplined". According to May's notes, he said:

> She has clear perception and sound judgement and is very just. Her judgements and attitudes are correct—sound—as I told her in regard to her attitude toward the government in Germany. You must be very happy—hopeful and assured. Remember all I have written you and Mary about her future—it will all be fulfilled—and attained. She has many years before her. You will be very happy—very proud of her—so will her Father.

Mary Maxwell at age 18

The Montreal Youth Group, circa 1930. Mary Maxwell seated on the floor, second from left

At Green Acre, Mary Maxwell in her Eskimo reindeer coat, in 1934, the year she gave a course on *The Dawn-Breakers*

The two cousins, Mary Maxwell and Jeanne Bolles, in Stuttgart, Germany, wearing the typical German national dress, the *dirndl,* 1936

II

Years of Marriage to Shoghi Effendi

II

Pilgrimage was a unique experience for every pilgrim. To sit at the dinner table with the "Sign of God on earth", to be able to ask him questions and receive his answers, these were bounties indeed beyond estimation. For May and Mary Maxwell, pilgrimage must have felt like an unexpected privilege, a glance from the grace of God after their lengthy sojourn in a Europe darkened by wars and rumours of wars. Their pilgrims' notes were among the most widely circulated at that time. Rúḥíyyih Khánum used to say that Shoghi Effendi allowed her to take down these notes in his presence and then correct them the following evening, for mother and daughter reviewed their notes each night, raising further questions of Shoghi Effendi if they had any doubts, so that no errors would be made. The Maxwell pilgrim notes are voluminous; Volume II alone is 37 pages long and bears a note by Rúḥíyyih Khánum: "The classifying under headings was done by me in order to keep the subjects often referred to together. R.R."

It was at the end of their pilgrimage that one day the mother of Shoghi Effendi asked to speak to May Maxwell and told her of Shoghi Effendi's offer of marriage to her daughter. Mary did not know of it until some weeks later. In reminiscing about those days, Rúḥíyyih Khánum used to say, with a twinkle in her eyes, that the beloved Guardian took her in hand and taught her Persian calligraphy after dinner in the course of those unforgettable evenings. He gave her a set of reed pens and ink and special mulberry papers and tutored her in the art of writing the Persian script. He also gave her a set of cards to copy from, on which the great calligrapher, Mishkín-Qalam, had written the Hidden Words of Bahá'u'lláh in three different styles of writing. In our early years in Haifa, she showed my husband and myself her copying note books in which Shoghi Effendi had himself written a line in his exquisite handwriting for her to copy underneath. She told us, "I could never copy his delicate script exactly, and the length of my sentence was always at least twice as long as his." And then she would add, with a bewitching smile, "I think Shoghi Effendi wanted an excuse to stay longer with me and to get to know me better!"

It was that time of the year when the mimosa trees were in full bloom and often, when she saw their golden showers in early spring, Rúḥíyyih Khánum would remember and speak of the day when the Guardian's younger sister came to her and said, "Shoghi Effendi wants to see you in his room." She had no notion of what was awaiting her, but on her way out of the Pilgrim House she broke a small branch of the mimosa flower and carried it with her into the presence of Shoghi Effendi and offered it to her beloved. That was the day he told her of his wish to marry her. Rúḥíyyih Khánum used to say, "I was alone with Shoghi Effendi for only 15 minutes before our marriage."

The wedding took place on March 24th, 1937, in Haifa. It was on this occasion that the beloved Guardian gave her the name Rúḥíyyih Khánum. May Maxwell, in a letter to her dear friend Leonora Holsapple (Armstrong), dated September 28th, 1938, gives us a glimpse of this unique event.

> As one might have expected, the Guardian's marriage was utterly simple, devoid of every earthly trapping, yet perfect in its beauty and simplicity. A few weeks after Rúḥíyyih Khánum and I arrived in Haifa, the Guardian with utmost

> gentleness began to teach her Persian and to give special attention to her general training and education. . . . Later, through conversations with his dear mother talking to me confidentially at his request (in the true oriental manner!) I was gradually informed, but at that time my daughter knew nothing about it, until the day, a week or two later, when the younger sister of the Guardian took her into his presence. Whatever happened at that time is known only to God, but He sustained and supported her in what was perhaps the most overwhelming shock of her life, with her deep reverence, almost worship of the Guardian as the Sign of God upon this earth. It was almost too much for a human being to bear. On March 24th the Guardian took Rúḥíyyih Khánum in his car to the tomb of Bahá'u'lláh where he chanted two prayers in the inner sanctuary and told her that that was the reality of the marriage. They were alone. When they returned, the Guardian's mother took them alone into the room of the Greatest Holy Leaf . . . Then all the families greeted and embraced them, the certificates of marriage were signed, and later Shoghi Effendi and his little western wife came to the Pilgrim House and it was our turn to embrace them and to feel all that it was possible to feel at such an overwhelming moment. There is no doubt about it that to us it was more like a dream than reality. The Guardian has shown her a love and kindness, an understanding and sympathy through which she is steadily developing, and although the tests are severe, Leonora, past all our comprehension, yet through the divine protection she is steadily attaining that station which God has ordained for her.

When Rúḥíyyih Khánum spoke of her wedding on certain occasions she used to say, as she also wrote in *The Priceless Pearl,* that on her wedding day, when she went with Shoghi Effendi to Bahjí, "I remember I was dressed, except for a white lace blouse, entirely in black for this unique occasion, and was a typical example of the way oriental women dressed to go out into the streets in those days, the custom being to wear black." The ring, which was a simple Bahá'í ring in the shape of a heart, had been given to her the day Shoghi Effendi proposed. He had asked her then to wear it on a chain around her neck, and on the day of their marriage, in the Shrine of Bahá'u'lláh, he took it from her and put it on her finger himself. It was a ring that had been given to Shoghi Effendi by the Greatest Holy Leaf, and Rúḥíyyih Khánum later had one made exactly like it for the beloved Guardian. They were both buried with their rings on their fingers. After the recital of the marriage vow, which took place in the room of the Greatest Holy Leaf, the mother of Shoghi Effendi placed Rúhíyyih Khánum's hand in the hand of her son, according to the old Persian tradition of "dast be dast". The witnesses were the father and the mother of the Guardian.

Rúḥíyyih Khánum often remarked that that evening with her parents present at the dinner table was not different from all the other evenings. It was only after dinner when Shoghi Effendi got up to leave that, as she used to say, "I followed him across the road to 'Abdu'l-Bahá's House and upstairs to his apartment." Her suitcase had been carried up already by Fujita, the Japanese Bahá'í serving Shoghi Effendi, earlier in the day.

The news of this blessed marriage electrified the Bahá'í world, both in the East and the West. Cables composed by the beloved Guardian and signed by his mother were sent to the National Spiritual Assembly of Iran and the National Spiritual Assembly of the United States and Canada. The one to the West, dated March 27th, 1937, read as follows:

> ANNOUNCE ASSEMBLIES CELEBRATION MARRIAGE BELOVED GUARDIAN STOP INESTIMABLE HONOUR CONFERRED UPON HANDMAID OF BAHA'U'LLAH RUHIYYIH KHANUM MISS MARY MAXWELL STOP UNION OF EAST AND WEST PROCLAIMED BY BAHA'I FAITH CEMENTED. [SIGNED] ZIAIYYIH, MOTHER OF THE GUARDIAN.

Later, responding to the congratulatory message of the above National Spiritual Assembly, Shoghi Effendi cabled:

> DEEPLY MOVED YOUR MESSAGE. INSTITUTION GUARDIANSHIP HEAD CORNERSTONE ADMINISTRATIVE ORDER CAUSE BAHA'U'LLAH ALREADY ENNOBLED THROUGH ITS ORGANIC CONNECTION WITH PERSONS OF TWIN FOUNDERS BAHA'I FAITH IS NOW FURTHER REINFORCED THROUGH DIRECT ASSOCIATION WITH WEST AND PARTICULARLY WITH AMERICAN BELIEVERS WHOSE SPIRITUAL DESTINY IS TO USHER IN WORLD ORDER BAHA'U'LLAH. FOR MY PART DESIRE CONGRATULATE COMMUNITY AMERICAN BELIEVERS ON ACQUISITION TIE VITALLY BINDING THEM TO SO WEIGHTY AN ORGAN OF THEIR FAITH.

Even the Montreal newspaper, "The Gazette", announced the marriage:

> Miss Mary Maxwell, only daughter of Mr. and Mrs. William Sutherland Maxwell, of Montreal, whose marriage to Shoghi Effendi Rabbani, Guardian of the Baha'i Faith, which took place in Haifa, Palestine, on Saturday last is announced. Mr. and Mrs. Maxwell were present at the ceremony. The bride and groom will live in Haifa, which is the centre of this faith. The groom is the grandson of Sir Abdul Baha Abbas and great-grandson of Baha'ollah, founder of the movement and formulator of its principles.

I myself remember, as a small child in Tehran, how much everyone rejoiced, how lavish were the banquets that were spread throughout the Bahá'í community in celebration of this wonderful event. It was like a fairy tale come true!

But the reality for Rúḥíyyih Khánum herself must have been far otherwise; the period of adjustment that followed for her was a training time which could not have been easy. Already, the circumstances, however propitious, were hardly conducive to tranquillity of spirit. To be parted at so great a distance from her beloved parents and say goodbye to her familiar life in Montreal, to be plunged into an oriental household together with all her in-laws under one roof, must have been hard for this young woman raised with a degree of freedom that was unusual even in the West at that time. Despite her natural buoyancy of temper and optimistic nature, she must have longed for and missed her parents terribly during these early years. In a letter to them she writes:

> Your love and the sense of your strength and courage sustain me in a way you cannot dream of . . . I have learned to be happy in a moment—to ride the waves. When the weather is calm I look around and enjoy everything. When a wave comes I go thro it as best I can and come out the other side!

It was especially hard at the beginning when she did not know the Persian language, for although the members of 'Abdu'l-Baha's family all spoke English, they communicated with each other in Persian. It was only natural, when comments were passed and jokes were shared which she did not understand, that she would have felt left out. Were it not for her beloved, Rúḥíyyih Khánum may well have been bereft.

But there were greater tests than mere loneliness and far greater trials than cultural isolation awaiting this young, naïve and open-hearted bride. Rúḥíyyih Khánum had a free and unsuspicious nature. She had entered this household with a sense of deep love, indeed almost veneration, for all who were related to Shoghi Effendi. What a blow it must have been so soon after her marriage to the Guardian, to first feel the winds of ill will blowing from the members of the household towards him, to recognize the signs of dissension harbouring within the bosom of his family towards the Centre of the Cause. She used to speak of those days with deep sorrow and pain. Many times we heard her say, "When I saw those oak trees fall one after another, I wept and prayed for my own soul, a mere blade of grass." For one by one, in those early years of her marriage, the family fell away from faithfulness; the branches of Afnán and Aghsán broke off from the mighty tree of the Covenant. They all left, one by one, until she was alone in that house at the side of her beloved. "Shoghi Effendi held me tight under his protective arms", she used to say.

She told us that during that first year of her marriage she suffered so much that one day she stood outside her room on the balcony and in deep distress said to herself, "I have reached the end of my tether." Her vivid imagination created a picture of her with a rope in her hand, herself at the bottom of the rope! Her sense of humour and her logical mind reminded her that, "Well, you are at the end of your tether, you cannot go down any farther, but you can climb up it!" From then on, she said, she never reached the end of her rope, as she could always climb up again.

She became the Guardian's shield and his sole support in those dark days of spiritual convulsion in the family of 'Abdu'l-Bahá. There was a time when Shoghi Effendi could not trust any member of his family to be alone with the Persian pilgrims for fear of the negative impact of their poisonous innuendoes and inferences. He would ask Rúḥíyyih Khánum to go down and sit with them. She told us that she had once been ill with jaundice, had had a fever and was as yellow as a canary, but despite this Shoghi Effendi sent her down to sit with the Persian women pilgrims. She could not go back up to bed until the last one had finally left. He was equally rigorous about strict attendance at all Holy Day celebrations and would tell Rúḥíyyih Khánum that if she felt indisposed, it would bring her healing to participate in these gatherings, which were in honour of the Central Figures of the Faith. It was also during this turbulent period that Shoghi Effendi pulled her up short one day, and gesturing to her hand, said, "Your destiny is in the palm of your own hand." This was a great shock for her and made her realize that she was not immune to her own tests of faith. "When Shoghi Effendi married me", she used to say, "I felt safe and smug and thought I had nothing more to worry about, my destiny was in his hand. But when he said that, there it was, back in my own hand." She would always make us laugh when she finished this very serious tale.

Her firmness in the Covenant, a manifestation of her deep faith, was her greatest protection in those early years of marriage. It was a suit of armour that preserved her spirit throughout her long life. During the year after Rúḥíyyih Khánum's marriage, May Maxwell wrote several letters to her young friend Marion Holley (Hofman) quoting her daughter's words:

> ". . . she says, "I am convinced that the greatest gift of a believer is faith; greater than intelligence, greater than character, for by faith we sink or swim, live or die, and it is almost the sole cause of our ultimate achievement and eternal life . . ." and ". . . she adds that she has learned

> how faulty her reasoning is, she rests everything on Faith. Faith is the keynote of her life, the solace and support of her existence, the foundation of her new-born character."

Perhaps the outpouring of her heart years later, in her poem "This is Faith", written on April 4th,1954, exemplifies the depth of her understanding of this subject.

THIS IS FAITH

To walk where there is no path
   To breathe where there is no air
To see where there is no light –
            This is Faith.

To cry out in the silence,
   The silence of the night,
And hearing no echo believe
   And believe again and again –
            This is Faith.

To hold pebbles and see jewels
   To raise sticks and see forests
To smile with weeping eyes –
            This is Faith.

To say: "God, I believe" when others deny,
   "I hear" when there is no answer,
"I see" though naught is seen –
            This is Faith.

And the fierce love in the heart,
   The savage love that cries
Hidden Thou art yet there!
   Veil Thy face and mute Thy tongue

Yet I see and hear Thee, Love,
Beat me down to the bare earth,
Yet I rise and love Thee, Love!
This is Faith.

Rúḥíyyih Khánum made frequent reference in later life to the fact that one of the reasons she had been chosen to be Shoghi Effendi's wife was because she was May Maxwell's daughter. We often heard her insist that he had told her so himself many times. Indeed, his own words emphasize this same theme and underscore it as one of the reasons for her unwavering faith:

> "She is imbued with the Bahá'í spirit," he is quoted as having said in May Maxwell's handwritten notes, "not confused or mixed with other matters—or subjects extraneous to the Cause . . . This is due to your influence—you do not realise to what extent Mary reflects your spirit. She is wholly devoted to the Faith—extremely attached."

In a letter to her mother, a year after her marriage, Rúḥíyyih Khánum wrote: "If anyone asked me what my theme was in life I should say, 'Shoghi Effendi'." It is clear from this that she had thrown herself, with heart and soul, into her destiny and her task required a rigorous discipline.

Although the faith on which it was reposed had been instilled within her since her birth and the love with which it was inspired had developed and evolved since her girlhood, her habits of schooling would not have seemed, at first glance, to have prepared her for such a destiny. But under Shoghi Effendi's strict tutelage she took herself in hand and applied herself to conscientious study. With what pride May Maxwell might have read the postscript in

Shoghi Effendi's own hand in his letter to her dated February 25th, 1939: "Mary is quite well, and exceedingly busy in her study of the Bible at present which I regard as a necessary foundation for her future work."

Rúḥíyyih Khánum used to relate a gleeful story on this subject of her study of the Bible. In the course of a conversation with Shoghi Effendi, she had one day said: "I have never read the Bible", to which Shoghi Effendi responded with surprise, "It is high time you did so!" Whereupon he gave her strict instructions to study it. She ended her story by saying, "After that, not only did I study the Bible diligently, but I also bought a copy of the Koran and read it from cover to cover before he found out that I had not read the Koran either!" Shoghi Effendi, in effect, was not only her theme in life, but also her education. Although she was an autodidact by nature and preferred to teach herself, rather than receive instruction—a habit she applied to many subjects in later life—he was, in effect, her principal teacher. At this time she was also seriously learning Persian. She used to say that Shoghi Effendi once told her, "I am a witness that all the Persian you have learned has been learned by you yourself, without any help."

One of the most outstanding services performed by Rúḥíyyih Khánum during those eventful twenty years at the side of the beloved Guardian, was to be his secretary. She undertook this task almost immediately after her marriage, and became his principal secretary in English from 1941 on. What may have been the first letter she wrote on behalf of Shoghi Effendi is addressed to her mother, and includes two postscripts in the handwriting of Shoghi Effendi. Characteristically, these serve to highlight the bond of unity the members of this family shared in their commitment to the Cause:

> The bond that has always united you to me has now been powerfully reinforced, and I feel sure that the services you will be enabled to render as a direct result of this new tie that binds us to each other will serve to draw me closer to you, and enable me to help you more effectively through my prayers.

The second states:

> Kindly assure Mr. Maxwell of my great love and affection for him. I have great hopes that he will in collaboration with you further the teaching work in Canada and thus pave the way for any international services he may be enabled to render in the future.

To her second letter written on behalf of Shoghi Effendi to her mother, Shoghi Effendi appends the following:

> Mary is in very good health and is making real progress in her spiritual life and is cultivating those virtues and traits of character that will be of immense value to her in her highly responsible and exalted task which she is strenuously striving to perform.

The reciprocity between Rúḥíyyih Khánum and her parents was preserved despite the difficulties of distance and separation. Following the guidelines set by Shoghi Effendi, she echoes the idea that service to the Cause performed by any one of them was a shared blessing for them all and of direct consequence to each. In an early letter to her father, responding to news of an indisposition on his part, she emphasizes the closeness between them with a characteristic jocularity that conceals her deeper anxieties and pains:

> So you see, Daddy, it is little short of a sacred obligation

> on your part to do everything to keep well and in that way and through serving the Cause help me all you can.

She adored her mother and had always hoped to see her again. Two years after her marriage, in December of 1939, May Maxwell echoes this theme of closeness which is sustained through service of the Cause, despite physical separation:

> . . . her sublime faith and courage, her deep insight into the true meaning of life and of the eternal fruits of human pain and sorrow, clearly reveal, not only the depth and strength of her character, but also . . . that she is walking in the path of light—that she is one of those rare few who have truly attained their highest destiny. It is not only thru my passionate love for this great Bahá'í Faith, but thru my love for her, and yearning to be more worthy of her, that I have considered going to South America to teach.

And so it was that May Maxwell decided to make her supreme sacrifice. She went travel-teaching in order to be more worthy of her beloved daughter whom she missed so much. She was 70 years old, with a weak heart and in very poor health. She arrived in Buenos Aires at the end of February, accompanied by her young niece, Jeanne Bolles, and the next day, on March 1st, 1940, she died of a massive heart attack.

The devastating news of May Maxwell's passing in Argentina was a terrible shock to Rúḥíyyih Khánum. She often repeated the story of how she received this sad news from the Guardian. Four cables had arrived that day and she took them to Shoghi Effendi in his study. He opened each one and then looked up at Rúḥíyyih Khánum with a mixture of shock, love and compassion on his face. She said the look frightened her, and she started backing away until she reached the wall. She said she wanted to sink into the wall so deep was the fear engendered in her by that look. Shoghi Effendi went over to her, held her in his arms and broke the news to her with great tenderness. He told her "Now I will be your mother". Then he spoke of the high station of May Maxwell in the Abhá Kingdom, of her joy in at long last having reached her heart's desire, of her nearness to her beloved Lord and Master, 'Abdu'l-Bahá. Then gently, in order to dispel her shaking grief, he began to talk to Amatu'l-Bahá in a lighter mood, to describe her mother's activities in the next world, where she was going and what she was doing in that sublime company. She would have been ushered immediately into the presence of Bahá'u'lláh first, of course, he assured her. And no sooner had she come there than she naturally asked permission to tell Him about her precious daughter. But she talked so much that Bahá'u'lláh had finally become tired and had passed her on to 'Abdu'l-Bahá. Here again she did nothing but talk about her beautiful daughter, until at length, exhausted, 'Abdu'l-Bahá passed her on to the Greatest Holy Leaf. And there she is still, said Shoghi Effendi laughing, there she is still talking about her beloved daughter, stopping every passing member of the Concourse with her opening lines, "Do let me tell you about my daughter . . . !" By the time he reached this point in his narrative, Rúḥíyyih Khánum was laughing through her tears. And so with infinite compassion and patience, he comforted her.

She went to the Shrine of Bahá'u'lláh afterwards and spent some time alone in that hallowed spot, reciting aloud the special prayer for burial. She loved this prayer and described its effect in these words:

> As I repeated the verses, 19 times each, each time it felt

like the rushing of a wave which enveloped me and washed away the burning in my heart and soul, until at the end I found peace and comfort.

The following three cables, the first from Shoghi Effendi to Mr. Maxwell and the last two from the Guardian and Rúḥíyyih Khánum herself to the National Spiritual Assembly of the United States and Canada, convey the significance of May Maxwell's station and the loving, generous act of Shoghi Effendi in inviting her bereaved husband to come and live close at last to his precious daughter.

> GRIEVED PROFOUNDLY YET COMFORTED ABIDING REALIZATION BEFITTING ONE SO NOBLE SUCH VALIANT EXEMPLARY SERVICE CAUSE BAHA'U'LLAH STOP RUHIYYIH THOUGH ACUTELY CONSCIOUS IRREPARABLE LOSS REJOICES REVERENTLY GRATEFUL IMMORTAL CROWN DESERVEDLY WON HER ILLUSTRIOUS MOTHER STOP ADVISE INTERMENT BUENOS AIRES STOP HER TOMB DESIGNED BY YOURSELF ERECTED BY ME SPOT SHE FOUGHT FELL GLORIOUSLY WILL BECOME HISTORIC CENTRE PIONEERS BAHA'I ACTIVITY STOP MOST WELCOME ARRANGE AFFAIRS RESIDE HAIFA STOP BE ASSURED DEEPEST LOVING SYMPATHY.

To the National Assembly he wrote:

> 'ABDU'L-BAHA'S BELOVED HANDMAID GATHERED GLORY ABHA KINGDOM. HER EARTHLY LIFE SO RICH EVENTFUL INCOMPARABLY BLESSED WORTHILY ENDED. TO SACRED TIE HER SIGNAL SERVICES HAD FORGED PRICELESS HONOUR MARTYR'S DEATH NOW ADDED. DOUBLE CROWN DESERVEDLY WON. SEVEN YEAR PLAN PARTICULARLY SOUTH AMERICAN CAMPAIGN DERIVE FRESH IMPETUS EXAMPLE HER GLORIOUS SACRIFICE. SOUTHERN OUTPOST FAITH GREATLY ENRICHED THROUGH ASSOCIATION HER HISTORIC RESTING-PLACE DESTINED REMAIN POIGNANT REMINDER RESISTLESS MARCH TRIUMPHANT ARMY BAHA'U'LLAH. ADVISE BELIEVERS BOTH AMERICAS HOLD BEFITTING MEMORIAL GATHERING.

Rúhíyyih Khánum's cable, dated March 4th, states:

> HUMBLY GRATEFUL BELOVED MOTHER ANSWERED GUARDIAN'S CALL TURNED SOUTHWARD SACRIFICED LIFE HOLY FAITH. BEG PRAYERS DAUGHTER MAY FOLLOW HER FOOTSTEPS.

Some months after the passing of May Maxwell, when Reza Shah Pahlavi of Iran was deposed and banished from his home and the news came that the Allies were planning to send him to Argentina, Shoghi Effendi told Rúḥíyyih Khánum, "Let the living dead go and visit the grave of the dead who are living."

One of the distinguishing characteristics of Rúḥíyyih Khánum was her selfless compassion for others in the midst of her own grief and sorrow. This letter written to Lucienne Migette, reveals her empathy towards this French Bahá'í, one of the many spiritual children of May Maxwell, who was extremely attached to her:

> I long to write to you in French as I know it is a closer bond to be addressed in one's own language at such a time and I speak French—<u>but I cannot spell it, alas</u>! But we do not even need words to express to each other what we feel!
>
> Indeed, in spite of my own grief at hearing my beloved had left me in this world, I was very distressed when I thought of how great a blow this would be to you! I know only too well how much you miss her! But now, dear sister, we must take comfort together. We must inherit, as her true children, the children of her radiant and beautiful soul, her character. We must be courageous as she was, going on to serve our beloved Faith even as she did, till the last breath of her life! I believe this is our heritage from her. To follow in her footsteps, to go on with work she never deserted, day or night, for over forty years! Only in this way can we be assured of being with her in the world to

> come. And I am sure Lucienne, that those who love her as we do, are only thinking of how to be with her again! . . .
>
> The beloved Guardian has been so kind to me, so loving and gentle. He has carried me over the abyss! It was so sudden, such a terrible shock! I was just living to see her again—but God takes away from us in order to bestow something greater. If Mother had been with me—she would not have died in Buenos Aires, sacrificing her life itself for the Faith, setting us all an example we long to follow, and winning the crown of Martyrdom!! We can only thank God we had her for a spiritual mother—for that is the eternal bond that cannot be severed!

The passing of May Maxwell marked the beginning of turbulent years in the Holy Land. The terrors of World War II were unleashed at this very hour, and every member of Shoghi Effendi's family had left the Cause. Mr. Maxwell had joined the Guardian and Rúḥíyyih Khánum in Rome in the summer of 1940, and when they could not return to Palestine, they only just managed to reach France and cross over to England on the last boat before the German army closed the borders. Since Rúḥíyyih Khánum recounts this story in full detail in *The Priceless Pearl*, I will only outline it briefly.

Although it was at the height of the "Children's evacuation" from Britain and all the boats were full, they were eventually able to get passage on the SS *Cape Town Castle* and the three of them sailed to South Africa in order to travel back up north to the Holy Land, via Egypt. This was Rúḥíyyih Khánum's introduction to sub-Sahara Africa and served as the main stimulus for her return there so many years later. They left Mr. Maxwell in Durban from where he flew to Khartoum in the Sudan, and Shoghi Effendi and Rúḥíyyih Khánum drove overland from Cape Town to Cairo, seeing some of the well-known sights along the way. In Rhodesia (now Zimbabwe) they visited Cecil Rhodes' grave and saw the magnificence of the Victoria Falls. When their car broke down on an isolated jungle path in the Congo Rúhíyyih Khánum asked Shoghi Effendi if she could go for a little walk while it was being repaired. She was longing to stretch her legs after hours of motoring and walked off down the narrow jungle path, oblivious of time, drinking in the beauty of untouched nature. Suddenly she was overtaken by an African cyclist who told her that the gentleman in the car was very worried over her. Glancing at her watch, Rúḥíyyih Khánum was shocked to realize she had been walking for almost two hours! She asked the man to lend her his bicycle and then cycled back as fast as she could to relieve the Guardian of his anxiety! Rúḥíyyih Khánum's adventurous spirit was one of her most endearing characteristics, especially in travelling. She loved the world of nature, trees nourished her eyes and soul, and she was never happier than when exploring. In later years she had the opportunity to satisfy this deep yearning for nature in her extensive travels.

The war years were filled with activity and great achievements at the World Centre. Before the arrival of Mr. Maxwell, Rúḥíyyih Khánum used to help Shoghi Effendi by making drawings to scale, and constructing paper and cardboard models of stairs in the Shrine Gardens, for example. She used to say that although Shoghi Effendi had a perfect sense of taste and proportion, he said he could not visualize an object; he had to see it in a drawing or a model. After Mr. Maxwell came to live in Haifa, Shoghi Effendi asked Rúḥíyyih Khánum to draw something for him one day, and she said, "But Shoghi Effendi, you have one of Canada's best architects across the street! Let him do it for you." He had looked up at her surprised, and asked, "Can your father do it?", to which she rejoined,

"Can he do it? He has built churches, hotels, parliament buildings, and numerous houses. This is child's play for him."

This was the beginning of what Rúḥíyyih Khánum liked to call a "partnership between the Guardian and my father." She would say, "My father was like a glove on the hand of Shoghi Effendi." It was during this period that Shoghi Effendi commissioned Mr. Maxwell to make the drawings for the superstructure of the Shrine of the Báb which was to be the crowning achievement of the latter's long and successful career. The love and collaboration between them was the greatest source of joy to Rúḥíyyih Khánum. She used to say, "I really learned to know and appreciate my father through Shoghi Effendi." She liked to tell the story of how, one night, when Shoghi Effendi was in bed resting, she had brought him a beautiful drawing of the main gate to the Shrine gardens. It was exquisitely drawn and delicately tinted with water colours. Shoghi Effendi had taken the drawing from her, looked at it, and said with a heavy sigh, "It is not fair." Alarmed, Rúḥíyyih Khánum had asked him what was wrong. "Nothing," he had said, "nothing is wrong; it is just that when you are given such a beautiful rendition, of course you want to have it!"

These were arduous but also very happy years for Rúḥíyyih Khánum. She used to say, "I was all alone: a wife, a companion, a secretary and the housekeeper." She was always the happiest when she worked the hardest. During this time she was also assisting the beloved Guardian as a proof reader after he completed the writing of his masterpiece, *God Passes By*. They would sit side by side, each holding several copies of pages typed by Shoghi Effendi, and for hours on end, they proof-read and transliterated those endless Persian names together. She said from the time she married until the Guardian's passing, she was always in the room with him when he composed messages, both in English and Persian. He composed out loud, and always chanted the Persian in his heavenly voice. For years after she treasured the pile of finished as well as unfinished embroidery which she used to sew during those hours.

At the end of World War II, the factional fighting between the Arabs and Jews began and the British Mandate came to an end with the Israeli War of Independence. The shortage of food and lack of help undermined Rúḥíyyih Khánum's natural good health and left her ill with a persistent fever and cough. She was alone in the house, with her father and the beloved Guardian to tend for and no one to take care of her. One day Shoghi Effendi asked if she had any one she could call upon to come and look after her and she thought of her dear friend and spiritual daughter, Gladys Cotton, who was unmarried and very fond of her. With Shoghi Effendi's encouragement she invited Gladys to come, which she did, to their mutual advantage, for as it turned out, she later married her old friend Ben Weeden in the Holy Land. Gladys proved to be a great assistance to Rúḥíyyih Khánum and even more so to Shoghi Effendi.

From 1941, when Rúḥíyyih Khánum became Shoghi Effendi's principal secretary, until 1957, she wrote thousands of letters on his behalf, a great many of which have already been published. She always lamented the fact that her handwriting was not good and her spelling imperfect. She used to refer to her handwritten letters and say: "If you look at some of those letters, you will see that Shoghi Effendi, on reading over them, has put a cross over the t's, a loop over the l's, a dot over the i's, and made the a's look like a's and the o's look like o's!" She also made fun of her own spelling which was sometimes ingenious and occasionally outrageous. Since she was never sure of it, she would ask Shoghi Effendi for the correct spelling of words and one day, in humorous exasperation, he turned to her and said, "Before you came into my life I could spell; now you have confused me!"

She also frequently described how Shoghi Effendi trained her to be a good secretary. From 1941 until 1951, when he appointed the International Bahá'í Council, Rúḥíyyih Khánum wrote all the Guardian's letters long hand. She often suffered from writers' cramp in her arm and shoulder because of this and it was only after Ethel Revell, a member of the Council residing in Haifa, became her much-loved private secretary that she had any assistance in having these letters typed. In those early days of training, Shoghi Effendi would tell her exactly what to write but when she showed him the finished letter he would take one look at its length, tear it up, and say, "Brief! Be brief!" She used to say with a chuckle that she quickly learned her lesson. In the early years, he would write down the points he wanted her to incorporate in pencil at the bottom of the letter he had received, but later on, when he saw how well she wrote, he would just tell her what to answer verbally. However, she always stressed the fact that he read every single letter she wrote for him before appending his own postscript. In later years, she wrote not only his personal letters but also his official correspondence with National Spiritual Assemblies. He also asked her to read the National Spiritual Assembly minutes received in German as he did not know that language. Needless to say, she was able to lift a tremendous load from his shoulders by performing this secretarial work.

In April of 1948, when Canada formed its first independent National Spiritual Assembly, Rúḥíyyih Khánum rejoiced with and for the Canadian Bahá'í Community. She truly participated with the Canadian friends in the celebrations, and through her loving messages encouraged and uplifted them. To Rosemary Sala, a very dear and old family friend, she cabled, on behalf of her father and herself:

> WE WOULD DEEPLY APPRECIATE YOUR MAKING ARRANGEMENT SERVE DELEGATES FRIENDS EITHER A BANQUET OR BUFFET IN OUR HOME TOKEN MAXWELL JOY OCCASION CONVENTION . . . DEEPEST LOVE. [SIGNED] RUHIYYIH

To which, three days later, Rosemary replied:

> HUNDRED FRIENDS OVERJOYED ACCEPT RIDVAN SUPPER SUNDAY YOUR GUESTS WONDERFUL SPIRIT MOUNTING HEALING TROUBLED HEARTS. DEEPEST LOVE. [SIGNED] ROSEMARY

To the Canadian National Convention she wrote:

> OUR HEARTS WITH YOU ALL JOYOUS TRIUMPHANT OCCASION LAUNCHING CANADIAN INDEPENDENT SERVICE BELOVED FAITH ASSUMPTION PRECIOUS RESPONSIBILITY. MAY YOUR LABOURS BREAK ALL RECORDS CARRY OFF ALL PALMS LOVING GREETINGS BEST WISHES ALL IN WHICH MAY SURELY JOINS US. [SIGNED] RUHIYYIH SUTHERLAND

The jubilant answer of the Convention reads as follows:

> YOUR MAGNIFICENT LETTER READ FIRST MORNING MEMORABLE CONVENTION FRIENDS DEEPLY GRATEFUL STIRRED REJOICE IN LINK WITH YOU AND YOUR UNIQUE DEVOTED SERVICES GLORIOUS FAITH. SEND LOVE AND PRAYERS. [SIGNED] FIRST CANADIAN CONVENTION.

The magnificent letter in their cable refers to a six-page typed letter signed "Rúḥíyyih Khánum", addressed "To the Delegates and friends attending the First Canadian National Bahá'í Convention".

Two weeks later, on May 10th, 1948, she received this loving cable from Dorothy Baker, who represented the United States National Spiritual Assembly at the inaugural Canadian Convention:

> TWO CONVENTIONS GLORIOUS YOUR MESSAGE CANADA READ MAXWELL HOME UPLIFTED ALL HEARTS STOP SUPPLICATING SPEEDY REOPENING COMMUNICATION OUR BELOVED PRAYING ACCEPTED RANSOM HIS SAFETY DEAREST LOVE. [SIGNED] DOROTHY BAKER

While the establishment of independent National Spiritual Assemblies was the cause of celebration in the Bahá'í world, the cause of political independence was the source of much bloodshed among nations at this time. In *The Priceless Pearl* Rúḥíyyih Khánum refers in full to the subject of war in the Holy Land prior to the formation of the State of Israel. This cable from the Bolles family, in April 1948, shows how concerned their family and friends must have been: "Guardian you all constantly mind heart praying safety peaceful surroundings . . ." Rúḥíyyih Khánum's cable to Milly Collins, again in April 1948, also gives us an idea of how the situation must have been, how uncertain the future was: "Written you letter but unlikely can mail it sorry. Very close to you always dearest. All well love. [signed] Ruhiyyih". Despite the fact that it seemed, at times, as if the tents of Armageddon were pitched in the valley of 'Akká while gunfire echoed between sea and mountain, Rúḥíyyih Khánum remained calm in the heart of the storm with Shoghi Effendi as her example.

Rúḥíyyih Khánum told us that Shoghi Effendi encouraged her to write, and once, as she was copying her own favourite poems in a book, he asked to see them for himself. The next day he gave her book back, saying, "I read them all. They are beautiful, they made me cry." She also said that after the transfer of the remains of the Purest Branch and his mother, Navváb, from the old 'Akká cemetery to Haifa and their interment on the slopes of Mt. Carmel next to the resting-place of the Greatest Holy Leaf in a very deeply moving ceremony, that night Shoghi Effendi looked at her and asked her, "Are you going to write an article about this?" She was surprised and said, "Oh, Shoghi Effendi, do you want me to?" He said, "Yes, it would be very good." The result was that moving and heart-rending article in volume VIII of *The Bahá'í World* entitled "The Burial of the Purest Branch and the Mother of 'Abdu'l-Bahá". His encouragement was the main reason she wrote the book *Prescription For Living*. She often said she felt so sad for the young men who returned, confused and disillusioned, from that devastating World War II to a changed and unfamiliar world. She wanted to give them some light, some direction, and a way to see hope for the future. She also used to say that David Hofman, who had just started his publishing company, George Ronald, encouraged her to write a book and let him publish it. After it came out, in 1950, she dedicated the first copy to the beloved Guardian. He read it, praised it and found one mistake in it that was later corrected; it is now translated into six languages. Through Shoghi Effendi's training, she also became an avid newspaper reader and kept interesting clippings to the end of her life.

The general suffering at this time was augmented in Rúḥíyyih Khánum's private life by her father's severe illness during the 1940s. In 1950, when they were in Europe for the summer, Gladys Weeden wrote to Rúḥíyyih Khánum from Haifa saying that the rationing of food was very bad and that given her father's serious condition and his complications of the gall bladder, she should know that fresh food was not available. So after consultation with the Guardian, it was decided that Mr. Maxwell should be sent to Canada with his Swiss nurse, until the situation improved in Israel. When they parted at the end of that summer, it was the last time Rúḥíyyih Khánum saw her dear father. He died two years later in Montreal.

After the formation of the State of Israel, Rúḥíyyih Khánum enjoyed a degree of freedom in Haifa that had not been possible for her before. Her social life became more varied and lively. She was a close friend of the Mayor of Haifa, Mr. Abba Khoushy, and his wife Hanna, and began to give wonderful dinner parties and soirées for the dignitaries of Haifa. She used to say Shoghi Effendi allowed her to entertain as long as it did not interfere with her work and she did not expect him to attend! She would hold her parties in the Western Pilgrim House in the company of the members of the International Bahá'í Council. This way, she said, the absence of the host was less obvious.

The Bahá'í world was stirred to great excitement in 1951 with the announcement of the formation of the first International Bahá'í Council, of which Rúḥíyyih Khánum was herself a member. She was also its chosen liaison with the Guardian. This news was announced to the Bahá'í world by Shoghi Effendi in a stirring message, dated January 9th, 1951, whose vital significance can be gauged by the fact that it is quoted in full in *The Priceless Pearl*.

A year later, in 1952, after the passing of Sutherland Maxwell, Shoghi Effendi sent a cable dated March 26th to the National Spiritual Assembly of the United States announcing that "mantle Hand Cause now falls shoulders his distinguished daughter Amatu'l Baha Ruḥiyyih who already rendered still rendering manifold no less meritorious self sacrificing services World Centre Faith Baha'u'llah".

And the following year both the Canadian and American "Bahá'í News" confirmed that "The Maxwell home, blessed by the Master's visit in 1912, has been declared a Shrine, to become to Bahá'ís, the most holy spot in Canada, surpassing even the future temple" This was not only one of the greatest gifts bestowed by 'Abdu'l-Baha on the Canadian Bahá'í community, but it was also a recognition of the unique services of three of Bahá'u'lláh's outstanding servants—William Sutherland, May and Mary Maxwell.

On the 15th of December 1952, the beloved Guardian announced that five Intercontinental Conferences would be held during the course of the Holy Year 1953, and designated Rúḥíyyih Khánum to be his representative at the Conference in Wilmette. It was a soul-stirring cable which not only offered the Bahá'ís a sweeping vista of their history and the challenges they faced ahead but also specifically enumerated Amatu'l-Baḥá's functions. She was, in his words, to

> DELIVER MY OFFICIAL MESSAGE ASSEMBLED BELIEVERS ELUCIDATE CHARACTER PURPOSES IMPENDING DECADE-LONG SPIRITUAL WORLD CRUSADE RALLY PARTICIPANTS ENERGETIC SUSTAINED ENTHUSIASTIC PROSECUTION COLOSSAL TASKS AHEAD.

She was furthermore delegated by him to dedicate the Mother Temple in North America on his behalf and

> UNVEIL OCCASION COMPLETION CONSTRUCTION MOTHER TEMPLE WEST PRIVILEGED ATTENDANTS WILMETTE CONFERENCE MOST PRIZED REMEMBRANCE AUTHOR FAITH NEVER BEFORE LEFT SHORES HOLY LAND TO BE PLACED BENEATH DOME CONSECRATED EDIFICE STOP MOREOVER ASSIGNING HER TASK ACT MY DEPUTY HISTORIC

With her beloved father, William Sutherland Maxwell,
in Torquay, England, 1948

Amatu'l-Bahá Rúḥíyyih Khánum, accompanied by the Hand of the Cause Amelia Collins, at the United States National Convention, 1953

Amatu'l-Bahá Rúḥíyyih Khánum, escorted to the United States National Convention by the Hand of the Cause Horace Holley, 1953

Amatu'l-Bahá on the occasion of the Dedication of the House of Worship in Wilmette, Illinois, 1953

Outside the door of her home at 1548 Pine Avenue West, Montreal, Canada, 1953

Rúḥíyyih <u>Kh</u>ánum in her family home in Montreal, Quebec, 1953

Amatu'l-Bahá standing beside a model of the Bahá'í House of Worship in Wilmette, in her home in Montreal, 1953

The first visit of Amatu'l-Bahá Rúḥíyyih Khánum to the grave of her beloved father, William Sutherland Maxwell, Montreal, 1953

CEREMONY MARKING OFFICIAL DEDICATION HOLIEST MASHRIQUL-ADHKAR BAHAI WORLD REARED EVERLASTING GLORY HONOUR MOST GREAT NAME HEART NORTH AMERICAN CONTINENT [SIGNED] SHOGHI

When the National Spiritual Assembly of the United States asked her if she would accept to be one of the keynote speakers at the Conference, she naturally accepted. When Shoghi Effendi heard of it, he asked her, "Can you do it?" Rúḥíyyih Khánum's response was utterly characteristic. "If I haven't got something to tell the Bahá'ís after 16 years at your side", she told him, "then I have not been worthy of this honour." She was by nature courageous, although her humility was also instinctive. And her love of Shoghi Effendi tempered her every response. She had a capacity, even at times of great stress, to keep her heart centred on the Covenant, her eyes fixed bravely ahead and her feet firm on the ground.

I came to the Holy Land as a pilgrim in Riḍván of 1953, and remember that Amatu'l-Bahá left for Wilmette a day before my pilgrimage ended. I will never forget how nervous and anxious she was then. She had left North America 18 years before, when she was a young Bahá'í and was known as the daughter of May Maxwell. Now she was returning as Amatu'l-Bahá Rúḥíyyih Khánum, the consort of the beloved Guardian and a Hand of the Cause of God. But she was equal to the challenge. Though very young myself, I was, like all who met her, struck at once by her innate grace, her regal presence and disarmed by her spontaneous vitality, her direct, unflinching gaze. She had eyes that shifted colour with her clothes, sometimes appearing to be green and sometimes blue. She herself always called them "yellow eyes" and when she turned her unwavering look at you, it was not easy to remain unaffected. In Wilmette, she rose to speak like the queen she was, her delicate, gauzy mantilla framing her lovely young face, and even from the photographs it is easy to see how she would have made an unforgettable impression on the Bahá'ís, as well as on the non-Bahá'í seekers and distinguished speakers. When the chairman introduced her, scattering much flattery and many flowers of rhetoric in the process, she quipped, "After such an introduction I should be lowered from heaven!" It brought the house down!

There were 2,000 believers gathered for the dedication of the Temple in Wilmette and Rúḥíyyih Khánum shook hands with all of them, developing a blister on her hand in doing so. She told us how she kept this sore fresh on her finger by turning her ring daily and pressing it hard against the flesh for almost three weeks, until she arrived back in Haifa. Then she showed it to the Guardian and said, "Look at this, Shoghi Effendi. There were so many Bahá'ís present that I got a blister."

After attending the 1953 Forty-fifth Annual Convention, the Bahá'í Dedication of the Temple, and the public Dedication the next day, she attended the All-America Intercontinental Conference from May 3rd to May 6th. In a cable answering one of Milly Collins', Shoghi Effendi states:

> REJOICE AMATU'L-BAHA'S SUCCESS SERVITUDE HOLY THRESHOLD SHARE YOUR PRIDE CONTINUED PRAYERS SURROUNDING YOU BOTH.

Rúḥíyyih Khánum was accompanied all through this trip by Amelia Collins, a Hand of the Cause and Vice-President of the International Bahá'í Council. From the United States they went to Montreal to visit her father's resting-place, which led Shoghi Effendi to send the following instructions to the Local Spiritual Assembly of Montreal:

> OCCASION VISIT AMATU'L-BAHA MONTREAL ADVISE ALL FRIENDS GATHER GRAVE HAND CAUSE SUTHERLAND MAXWELL PAY TRIBUTE HIS IMMORTAL SERVICES WORLD CENTRE FAITH STOP INSTRUCTING AMATU'L-BAHA MILLY PLACE BLOSSOMS SHRINE AND FRESH FLOWERS MY BEHALF STOP APPRECIATE PHOTOGRAPH ASSEMBLED FRIENDS LOVE.

He asked Rúḥíyyih Khánum to buy $120.00 worth of flowers on his behalf for this event, and specifically requested that most of them be blue. He knew Sutherland Maxwell's favourite colour was blue. The memorial gathering was held at the graveside on May 10th and that evening Rúḥíyyih Khánum spoke at a public meeting at the Ritz-Carlton Hotel.

After all these duties, she had the painful task of sorting out her parents' belongings, and with Shoghi Effendi's consent, shipped her personal furniture to Haifa. She then did a beautiful thing that pleased the Guardian immensely. She gave her home, "The Bahá'í Shrine", at 1548 Pine Avenue West, to the Faith. It is now registered in the name of the National Spiritual Assembly of Canada.

When she finally returned to the Holy Land, she found Shoghi Effendi waiting for her at the top of the staircase, in their own private apartment in the Master's House. He was so thrilled with her achievements on this trip that he had prepared a special gift for her homecoming and handed her his gift right there on the stairs. Years later, she showed me the exquisite tooled-leather folder which framed two beautiful sheets of illuminated paper inscribed by Shoghi Effendi's own hand. He had written in English on one side and in Persian on the other, and the gist of the words were something like: "Welcome Amatu'l-Bahá, welcome. You return victorious in discharging your manifold duties. Your martyred mother and your saintly father are proud of you, and your Guardian is well pleased with you." These are naturally not the Guardian's own words, but just what I remember of them.

The last years of our beloved Guardian's life were unusually busy for Amatu'l-Bahá. The International Archives Building was being constructed and Shoghi Effendi had begun to buy the appropriate furnishings for it during his summers in England. With Rúḥíyyih Khánum's help he searched for and found all the ornaments and cabinets needed to house the precious relics of the Faith. Rúḥíyyih Khánum would often say, "Shoghi Effendi was the hunter and I was his hunting dog." She would go out and look for what he needed, and whenever she found the appropriate object, she would come and tell him about it. Then they would go together and if he liked the object, he would purchase it.

She once asked Shoghi Effendi for a piece of land on the grounds of their home to make a garden of her own and he offered her a little corner at the back of the house to do with as she pleased. This she worked on with great enthusiasm, making a plan for a fish pond and flower beds which when completed transformed the patch into a beautiful little garden. When Shoghi Effendi was buying eagles to ornament the Shrine gardens, she found a small stone eagle herself, and since he agreed that she might have it, she placed her own eagle on the roof of a little building by her pool and garden. During this time too, and usually till quite late at night, which was her only free time, she designed and decorated the three rooms in the Master's House which Shoghi Effendi had given to her to furnish with her Montreal furniture. 'Abdu'l-Bahá's House was extremely austere. They had been prisoners and exiles and had accumulated no furniture of any value. Only the Master's drawing room, where He received non-Bahá'í officials at the end of His life, was furnished by the Greatest Holy Leaf with a set of matching chairs and divans which she had bought in Beirut. Now that Rúḥíyyih Khánum had her own furniture, she began to make this home her own. She created an exquisite library which she later used for special dinner parties, particularly for dignitaries, and she called her beautiful drawing room "Montreal in Haifa".

From 1952 onwards, when some degree of safety and order was restored to Israel, Shoghi Effendi re-opened the opportunity for pilgrimage, and the friends, deprived for a period of over ten years, started coming to the Holy Land in groups of nine, from both the East and the West. To welcome them, to cater to their needs, and respond to their concerns was a considerable task in itself which consumed not only many hours of the Guardian's time but those of Rúḥíyyih Khánum as well. All three meals for both Pilgrim Houses, East and West, as well as for the domestic help, were prepared in the kitchen of 'Abdu'l-Bahá's House and it was Rúḥíyyih Khánum who had to plan for and prepare these unending meals in the face of great shortages of all kinds of essential foods in the post-war years.

In 1957, the beloved Guardian and Rúḥíyyih Khánum left together for their summer vacation for the last time. The Guardian was very tired. As usual, he maintained all his correspondence in his absence and carried with him all his notes for his map of the Ten Year Crusade, which was approaching its midway point. In August that year he thrilled the Bahá'ís of the world with a two-fold message. The first part was the announcement of five Intercontinental Conferences to celebrate this midway point of the Crusade, and the second was his appointment of eight more Hands of the Cause in different continents. Everyone was filled with anticipation. Everyone looked forward to jubilation and celebration ahead. We in Uganda were thrilled beyond belief, for we had learned with awe and excitement that our precious Amatu'l-Bahá Rúḥíyyih Khánum had been designated by the beloved Guardian to represent him at the African Conference in Kampala. She was going to come to us!

And then, on November 4th, the cataclysmic news of Shoghi Effendi's passing rocked the Bahá'í world. He had died in London, we heard in disbelief, and was gone from amongst us. The community of the Greatest Name, which had for thirty-six years looked to him for guidance, for encouragement, for leadership and, above all, for his encompassing love, was lost, and bereft. And there was no one to turn to but Amatu'l-Bahá, though she was the most forlorn of all at that time. Her mother, whom she adored, had died far from her side, and her father, whom she so cherished, was gone too, and now she had lost her Guardian who had replaced them both. Her own heart-wrenching story, entitled "The Passing of Shoghi Effendi", written soon after his death, tells us everything that could be told. And yet, we will never know what she must have felt in her soul on that cold November morning in a hotel bedroom when she found her beloved gone. She was alone, and as far as she knew the Guardian had left no will. It was up to her to take the next step to ascertain what should be done.

III

Final Years of Service and Travel

The time foreordained unto the peoples and kindreds of the earth is now come. The promises of God, as recorded in the holy Scriptures, have all been fulfilled. Out of Zion hath gone forth the Law of God, and Jerusalem, and the hills and land thereof, are filled with the glory of His Revelation. Happy is the man that pondereth in his heart that which hath been revealed in the Books of God, the Help in Peril, the Self-Subsisting. Meditate upon this, O ye beloved of God, and let your ears be attentive unto His Word, so that ye may, by His grace and mercy, drink your fill from the crystal waters of constancy, and become as steadfast and immovable as the mountain in His Cause.

Baha'u'llah
Gleanings from the Writings of Baha'u'llah, p. 12

III

The devastating shock of the sudden passing of beloved Shoghi Effendi remained with Amatu'l-Bahá throughout her life. She told me more than once, usually at times of sad despondency, which were rare, that on that terrible morning when she went towards his bed and greeted him as usual, when she received no answer and touched him, when she found him cold and realized with a stab of pain that he was gone, her instant reflex was to kill herself. She said that such a state of mind and heart did not last long, however, for she knew only too well that he would not be pleased with her if she had done this. He had trained her for twenty years and entrusted his affairs to her hands. How could she fail him now, at that moment of distress? In the early years when we came to Haifa, Ali and I heard her say several times that during their last summer in London, Shoghi Effendi had on one occasion told her, "I don't want to go back to Haifa, you go alone, you know what to do." She said that at the time she had attributed this statement to his extreme tiredness and despondency, as he was ill with severe influenza. But later when she remembered his words, it gave her courage and self-assurance. The fulfilment of all his hopes and the completion of all his aspirations for the Ten Year Crusade became of uppermost importance to her. His good pleasure became the goal and object of her existence. From that moment to the end of her life her priorities never wavered.

In the face of her own immeasurable personal loss, however, it is remarkable to consider with what self-abnegation her heart turned to her fellow believers at that critical time of trial, with what heroism, courage and compassion she became the lighthouse to guide and show us the way to safety. She appealed with all her soul to the unseen Source of life and light, and then set about doing what needed to be done. All around her, friends were prostrate with grief, helpless with sorrow, leaving her to rise alone to the painful task in front of her, for the sake of her beloved Shoghi Effendi. She had to inform the Hands of the Cause and the Bahá'í world of this tragic event in such a manner as might lessen as much as possible the shock waves it was bound to cause. She had to tell the heart-broken believers to come to his funeral and bid their Guardian a last farewell. She went around London looking for a befitting burial ground and found it. She searched for a shroud and chose the casket and bought it. She saw to every detail in the sad days that followed. And the day after the funeral, when she was driving away from the graveside, she saw in her mind's eye a vision of a column, an eagle and a globe, and she conceived the monument above his grave. She remembered how fond Shoghi Effendi had been of beautiful columns, and how he had said it was a pity that in his gardens there was no place for a single column. With this thought in mind, she designed the graceful column rising over his grave and placed the globe on it, surmounted by the symbol of his victories: the majestic eagle, with its wings open. Was it ready to fly?—Or had it perhaps just alighted from its lofty heights?

On the 15th of November Rúḥíyyih Khánum arrived in Haifa, accompanied by her dear friend and colleague, the Hand of the Cause Milly Collins. Three days later the first Conclave of the Hands of the Cause began in Bahjí. It was during the first days of this Conclave that they searched for the will of Shoghi Effendi and did not find it. At the end of that historic meeting, the Hands of the Cause informed the benumbed community of the Most Great Name that there was no other recourse but to turn with heart and soul to the explicit directives in *The Dispensation of Bahá'u'lláh*, which Shoghi Effendi had referred to as his Will and Testament, to complete the goals of the Ten Year Crusade which he had bequeathed to them before he died, and to arrange for the election of the Universal House of Justice at the end of that period, the only infallible source of guidance for the future.

During that first year after Shoghi Effendi's passing, Rúḥíyyih Khánum spent most of her time in Bahjí and slept in the Mansion. Apart from carrying out all her heavy administrative duties, she threw herself into physical work, cleaning the Shrine and working in the gardens. She could not bear the emptiness and the loneliness of her apartment in Haifa. The next five or six years were perhaps the saddest and hardest in her entire life. Her *Poems of the Passing* are the best witness to her broken heart. The first poem of this collection, "A Waste, a Waste the World to Me" was written on December 2nd, barely a month after the beloved Guardian's passing.

The messages of the Hands of the Faith written during this period give us a glimpse of the back-breaking responsibility which these brave men and women so ably shouldered in protecting the Cause of God and leading the Bahá'ís of the world to their final victory. The Hands of the Cause who gathered together at their Conclaves were strong individuals from both the East and the West. Their primary aim and objective was to direct and hold together the affairs of the Cause of God but there often seemed to be unfathomable gaps in their conflicting points of view. Mr. Samandarí, the oldest and one of the most respected and loved among the Hands, used to say that the role

Amatu'l-Bahá played in those early gatherings was vital. She became the bridge between cultures and languages, a Westerner imbued with Eastern understanding. Her horizons had been widened and stretched by Shoghi Effendi. As a result of her deep sense of fairness and her ability to see clearly both sides of any argument, the gaps were gradually narrowed and negotiated.

Amatu'l-Bahá demonstrated her own, immediate commitment to service after the passing of the Guardian when she accepted to attend the first of the series of the Intercontinental Bahá'í Conferences called by the beloved Guardian to mark and celebrate the midway point of the Ten Year Crusade. Initially, her grief was so intense that she did not want to go, but her fellow Hands convinced her that since it had been the wish of Shoghi Effendi, she must do so. She travelled with Dr. Luṭfu'lláh Ḥakím, a member of the International Bahá'í Council, who had been designated by Shoghi Effendi to escort Amatu'l-Bahá on that trip. Her dear cousin Jeanne Chute with her husband Challoner also accompanied her. Although Rúḥíyyih Khánum was in mourning, and wore black for one year after Shoghi Effendi's passing in accordance with the custom of the East, she altered this custom for the duration of her trip to Africa and arrived at Entebbe Airport dressed beautifully in a simple white suit. She told me afterwards that all her clothes for that Conference had been seen and approved by the Guardian the previous summer, and this was one of the reasons why she did not come to Kampala in mourning clothes. She also wanted to create the sense of jubilation during this Conference the way Shoghi Effendi had anticipated it should be, and she knew that a mood of mourning would not allow for this. Her standard in life was always his approval and his good pleasure.

Over 900 people stood up in sorrowful awe as she entered that Conference Hall in Kampala, on January 24th, 1958. She was tall, erect and very beautiful. And then, 400 African Bahá'ís raised their voices and began to sing "Alláh-u-Abhá", softly and spontaneously. The air was so charged with love, so pent-up with emotion as Amatu'l-Bahá walked up the central aisle, that we were all shaken. We felt lifted to higher realms. When she stood before us to address the Conference, her voice broke and tears came to her eyes several times. But the waves of deep love and sympathy in that audience were tangible; they enveloped and caressed her, and at the end assuaged her sorrow. She often said the love of the friends, particularly the Africans, was like a balm to her soul and a healing for her grief at that time. She also said that Africa was the continent that brought most joy to the heart of Shoghi Effendi at the end of his life. That was why she chose to place the continent of Africa on the front of the globe surmounting his grave. Her love for the Africans and their continent became a permanent part of her life afterwards. She brought to that Conference a wider perspective, a global outlook, an all-embracing point of view that we had been lacking, and she went back from it recharged with hope and courage to continue.

Although she travelled to different conferences and to the Dedications of both Mother Temples of Africa and Australasia during the Custodianship of the Hands, her historic journeys for which she is best remembered by the friends did not begin until after the election of the Universal House of Justice. One of the most important trips during this interregnum period, however, was her visit to major communities in the United States and Canada in 1960. When Mason Remey made his idiotic self-appointed claim as Guardian, and sent word that he was going to attend the National Convention in Wilmette to proclaim himself to the Bahá'ís, the Custodians of the Faith asked Rúḥíyyih Khánum, who knew Mason from her earliest childhood, to be present at that occasion and protect the assembled friends from any negative influence that he might try to exert on them. Through her wisdom, her courage, her firmness in the Covenant, she was able to infuse and reinforce in the hearts of the friends the spirit of confidence and steadfastness.

In 1961, the election of the International Bahá'í Council took place. This Council, which was the precursor of the Supreme Universal House of Justice, was destined to be of great assistance to the Hands in the preparation for that first International Bahá'í Convention. It helped the Hands to compile the marvellous statistical booklet at the end of the Ten Year Crusade, as well as to make all the other logistical arrangements. One of the major decisions of the Hands during this period was that Rúḥíyyih Khánum should undertake the completion of the interior of the International Archives Building. Again, in order to complete this task she turned for assistance to the younger members of the newly elected Council. Shoghi Effendi had bought beautiful Chinese and Japanese furniture during the last year of his life for the purpose of decorating and displaying the holy relics, and these had to be carefully arranged and meticulously prepared for their precious contents. Artistry, a sense of proportion, a strict adherence to the placement of the objects according to the priority of their importance—all these guided Amatu'l-Bahá in her task. The following acknowledgement written by the Hands of the Cause in the Holy Land on August 28th, 1961, expresses the significance and the results of what she did:

In London, soon after the passing of Shoghi Effendi, 1958

Arriving at the Intercontinental Conference in Kampala, Uganda, January 1958

In Hopivilla, Arizona, during her tour of the United States in 1960. Amatu'l-Bahá Rúḥíyyih <u>Kh</u>ánum met with several Chiefs and Elders of the Hopi Tribe

Amatu'l-Bahá Rúḥíyyih <u>Kh</u>ánum's visit to the Peigan Reserve, Alberta, Canada, 1960. Here she is with the elders when Chief Charlie Crow Eagle officially conferred upon her the name *Natu Okcist*—"Blessed Mother"

At the Conclave of the Hands of the Cause in Bahjí, 1961. Amatu'l-Bahá Rúḥíyyih <u>Kh</u>ánum between Ṭarázu'lláh Samandarí and Enoch Olinga, Abu'l-Qásim Faizí and Paul Haney in the background

Amatu'l-Bahá chairing the first International Bahá'í Convention in the hall of the Master's House in Haifa, Riḍván, 1963

> We were so impressed by the effect that has been achieved in the Archives Building that we feel we should write to express to you our appreciation . . . The interior is truly worthy of the purpose for which the building was designed. Many generations of Bahá'ís will be grateful for the cumulative backbreaking efforts which were put into making the Archives Building a fitting place for the holy relics it will contain, though they may not be aware of the difficulties and strains under which the result was achieved.

The triumphant conclusion of the Ten Year Crusade of the beloved Guardian, in April of 1963, was crowned by the election of the long-awaited Universal House of Justice in Haifa. After consultation and with the approval of the Hands of the Cause, Amatu'l-Bahá arranged to conduct the opening session of this first International Bahá'í Convention in the House of 'Abdu'l-Bahá itself. It was highly symbolic that the election should take place in that blessed House, which had played such a significant role in the unfoldment of the Administrative Order of Bahá'u'lláh. With the help of some of the Council members, she painstakingly measured the central hall, as well as the four rooms opening into it, and confirmed that the space was just large enough for exactly the right number of chairs to seat all the attendants.

"The Most Great Jubilee" was truly unforgettable. How thrilling was that morning of the first election of the Universal House of Justice, and how great the celebration which followed it in Bahjí at the Shrine of the Blessed Beauty! To befittingly honour the occasion, Rúḥíyyih Khánum had ordered thousands of roses and carnations to carpet the inner rooms of all three Shrines. With just a handful of helpers she worked through the day and all through the night, till the early hours of dawn, nipping the buds and culling the blossoms to lay thick upon the ground. This lovely gesture was to become a tradition that would be followed in later years, and was an exquisite example of Rúḥíyyih Khánum's aesthetic and spiritual sensibilities combined. The beauty and the fragrance of the Shrines on that day were imprinted in the hearts and memories of all present. She opened that International Bahá'í Convention and every successive one, till that of April 1998.

After the successful election of the Supreme Body, Rúḥíyyih Khánum and the Hands of the Cause of God rejoiced with 7,000 Bahá'ís in London in the majestic Royal Albert Hall for the celebration of the first Bahá'í World Congress. It was on this occasion that the Universal House of Justice presented its very first statement to the Bahá'í world, in which tribute was paid to those who

> share(d) the victory with their beloved commander, he who raised them up and appointed them. They kept the ship on its course and brought it safe to port. The Universal House of Justice, with pride and love, recalls on this supreme occasion its profound admiration for the heroic work which they have accomplished . . . the reality of the sacrifice, the labour, the self-discipline, the superb stewardship of the Hands of the Cause of God.

Amatu'l-Bahá personally invited a number of indigenous Bahá'ís to attend this historic event as her personal guests, from Africa, South America and Australia. "Uncle" Fred, that dignified, old Aborigine from Australia, was among them and his stalwart faith was a source of joy and pride to her. Her deeply moving and thought-provoking talk on Shoghi Effendi's life on this occasion was a masterpiece of eloquence and poignancy. And none who saw her there could forget the emotions experienced as the dear friends from Africa softly chanted the rise and fall of "Alláh-u-Abhá" once more, just as they had done at the Kampala Conference after the passing of the Guardian. And none who heard them there could restrain the stab of loss and sorrow and the thrill of joy as we brought his Ten Year Crusade to its final and triumphal close.

Rúḥíyyih Khánum's systematic travels around the globe began in the year 1964. Many times, both privately and publicly, Rúḥíyyih Khánum would talk about the genesis of these unique trips. She would recount an incident in the lifetime of Shoghi Effendi, when one day, as he was passing by her desk, he stopped and looked at her and said, "What will become of you after I die?" She was shattered by this unexpected remark and began to weep, saying, "Oh Shoghi Effendi, don't say such terrible things. I don't want to live without you." He paid no attention, however, and after a pause continued, "I suppose you will travel and encourage the friends". She would say this was the only remark he ever made about what she should do with her life after his passing. And so it was that, when she was somewhat freed from her arduous administrative duties and the affairs of the Cause were placed under the infallible guidance of the Universal House of Justice, she took these words as his last instructions to her and did her utmost to fulfil his hopes.

In the course of her long life she travelled to 185 countries, dependencies and major islands of the globe. But while she visited just 31 countries in the first 54 years, she travelled in all the rest during her last years, from 1964 until her final trip in 1997. When I tried to count the number of territories she visited in these 34 years, I came up with the astounding figure of 154. Many of these countries were visited more than once, and some, like

India, were honoured by her presence as many as nine times.

But travelling was not the only thing she did during this period and her trips were of such a variety that the best way to look at them is through the range of activities which they involved. Indeed, the wide spectrum of her achievements, from 1964 until her last official engagement in April of 1998, leaves the mind reeling with disbelief. To stand back for a brief moment and look at all that she accomplished in 34 years dazzles the sight. Her many activities scintillate like multi-coloured rays of light reflected through a crystal window. The single-minded purity of that light was one: devotion to the Covenant; but its expression was infinitely varied, richly diverse. One is reminded of May Maxwell's words written to and about her beloved daughter many years ago:

> I really feel, Mary, that the great spiritual blessings which are coming to you in guiding so many souls to the Blessed Cause, are not only due to the power of spiritual attraction which 'Abdu'l-Bahá gave you, but also to your strict obedience to the instructions of Shoghi Effendi.

Though I was privileged to travel with her on some of her remarkable journeys during this time, I can only write of all that she accomplished in their course with my head bowed in admiration, acutely aware of my inadequacy to summarize her achievements. Amatu'l-Bahá Rúḥíyyih Khánum used to say, "I have lived five lives in this one life", and this remark could just as well apply to her trips, for she was certainly covering at least five times as many activities in the course of a single journey as any other normal traveller might have done.

In each country she performed multiple services for

the Cause. Her role as Ambassador of the Bahá'í Faith, for example, was remarkable in itself. Everywhere she went she met with Heads of State and high-ranking authorities at the national, local or even village levels, and moved with complete ease from one class of society to another. Although she herself was in every way queenly and worthy of honour and respect, she always approached these emblems of material power and political authority with deference and a natural humility. From the first moment of her audience, she would explain that her visit was in the nature of a courtesy call, and nothing more. She would invariably state that she had come from the World Centre of the Bahá'í Faith and was visiting the Bahá'ís in that country, who were a strictly apolitical and non-partisan people, well-wishers of the government and obedient to its laws. When asked by the National Spiritual Assemblies of these countries to raise the question of Bahá'í registration or make any other request during the course of her official audiences, she would always refuse. She would then explain to the Bahá'ís that her purpose in meeting any officials or dignitaries was to introduce them more intimately to the principles of the Faith and create an atmosphere of trust so that later on, when she had gone away, the Bahá'í institutions could more easily approach the government and make their own requests. This policy invariably worked.

In Africa alone she met with 17 Heads of State and was instrumental in helping the Bahá'ís achieve many of their legal goals. The highest in rank and the leader she most valued meeting in all her travels was Emperor Haile Selassie of Ethiopia. She greatly admired his nobility, his courage and his uprightness. The Head of State whose meeting brought her the greatest joy and pride was His Highness Malietoa Tanumafili II of Western Samoa, the first ruling monarch to embrace the Cause of Bahá'u'lláh. In all her encounters, she strove to be positive and looked for every opportunity to offer praise and appreciation in her dealings with state officials, even if very little was called for. When she met the Prime Minister of India, Indira Gandhi, for example, she praised her courage and high ideals and assured her of her prayers. No wonder that proud lady was touched and responded with warm respect and reverence. She always maintained a high standard of propriety in these matters, and when she shared the platform or sat at dinner with such people as Prince Philip of Great Britain or the Archbishop of Canterbury, with Governors-General and Ambassadors, she invariably won their admiration and respect, not only for herself but most importantly for the Cause of Bahá'u'lláh. This was her ultimate concern. Rúḥíyyih Khánum truly had no personal ambition; she was not in the least interested in meeting or moving in such company for its own sake or her pleasure. It was only for the Cause that she would accept any appointments and invitations of this kind.

Another activity which she undertook in the course of her many travels was contact with the representatives of the media. She must have had hundreds of newspaper, radio and television interviews, in the capital cities around the world as well as in the large and small towns of every country she visited. No matter where the interview took place, no matter how insignificant or important, she agonized over what she would say and never took the opportunity for granted. Before going to meet a journalist or be filmed in a studio she would always pray and ask for God's guidance, His assistance and, above all, His protection. She used to tell the friends that when they met the representatives of the media, their principal aim

The opening session of the World Congress in London, 1963 where Amatu'l-Bahá gave her unforgettable talk on Shoghi Effendi; Enoch Olinga was her chairman. Some of the Hands of the Cause and newly-elected Universal House of Justice members are in view

At the World Congress, London, England, 1963. Amatu'l-Bahá Rúḥíyyih Khánum with her dear friend "Uncle" Fred Murray, the Aboriginal Australian Bahá'í

Amatu'l-Bahá Rúḥíyyih Khánum with the Indian Prime Minister Indira Gandhi and Violette Nakhjavani, New Delhi 1967

Amatu'l-Bahá Rúḥíyyih <u>Kh</u>ánum with His Highness Malietoa Tanumafili II at the time of the dedication of the Mother Temple of the Pacific Ocean, Apia, Western Samoa, 1984

Presenting "The Promise of World Peace" on behalf of the Universal House of Justice to the Secretary-General of the United Nations Pérez de Cuellar, November 1985

H.R.H. The Prince Philip, Duke of Edinburgh, President of the World Wide Fund for Nature, receiving a copy of the Bahá'í Statement on Nature presented by Amatu'l-Bahá Rúḥíyyih Khánum, Switzerland, 1987

should be to create a good impression of the Faith. "If these people only remember one thing, that the word 'Bahá'í' means something good, you have achieved your purpose", she used to say. She would advise the friends to have enough printed information about the teachings and concepts of the Faith always available in advance as hand-outs, because the media representatives never remembered verbal information correctly. All they remembered was the impression they received. "Make every effort to make this worthy of Bahá'u'lláh", she urged the friends. Many of the articles that appeared after interviews with the press portrayed Rúḥíyyih Khánum's personal charm and candour. In a newspaper in Nigeria, for example, a cheeky young reporter wrote a very good article on the Bahá'í Faith, ending with this comment: "Madame Rabbani, you are always welcome in our country; next time you come please bring your daughter, who must be very beautiful"! So many times, either on radio or television, the interviewer would become so interested in Amatu'l-Bahá that he would increase the time allotted to her, on occasion by half an hour.

Another vital service rendered by Amatu'l-Bahá in the course of her many travels was her role as the representative of the Universal House of Justice at national and international Bahá'í Conferences across the planet. Her talks were both instructive and memorable on these occasions. Standing on platforms on behalf of the Sacred Institution she served, in the course of Bahá'í Conventions at Riḍván, at youth conferences and Native gatherings, at inaugurations of Bahá'í Temples and other great historical events to which the Bahá'ís had streamed from all the quarters of the globe, she was erect and regal and forever memorable, the essence of dignity and beauty. Her mastery of just the right word on each of these occasions, her ability to draw out her audience and touch people's hearts, her clear and simple logic which made sense to everyone alike, and, above all, her wit and her bewitching sense of humour—these qualities endeared her to and charmed her audiences. Who could ever forget her visible joy who saw her at New York City at the second Bahá'í World Congress? Who could forget her eloquence who heard her speak, in Paris, in Machu Picchu, or Auckland? Although Rúḥíyyih Khánum did not consider herself a pious person who spent much time in prayer, I believe she had a genuine reverence which was very private and unpretentious. When asked, she attributed her power of public speaking to the fact that at the beginning of her marriage Shoghi Effendi had recommended that she memorize the beautiful prayer of 'Abdu'l-Bahá which begins, "O Lord, my God and my Haven in my distress! My shield and my Shelter in my woes! . . ." and which concludes with the poignant sentence: "Loose my tongue to laud Thy name amidst Thy people, that my voice may be raised in great assemblies and from my lips may stream the flood of thy praise." She also attributed it to the advice given by 'Abdu'l-Bahá to May Maxwell, to turn her heart to Him, pray, and then speak, for Rúḥíyyih Khánum herself followed this advice faithfully. She gave talks with the same degree of resourcefulness in French, in German and in Persian. I remember when we were at a meeting with the Bahá'ís of Mauritius, she asked her audience whether they wanted to hear her French, which was grammatically rusty and a muddle of genders, or have her speak in English, with a translator? The whole audience, with one voice, begged her to speak in French and I, who understand the language most imperfectly, can testify to the impact of her words, despite the faults! Persian also was a language she had learned orally and by herself. She didn't know much grammar and her vocabulary was limited and rather quaint. Despite its limitations, however, she always knew exactly what she wanted to say, and said it forcefully, simply, choosing exactly the right words. The Persians, I know, just loved her ingenuity in inventing new words all of her own, a combination of the cross-fertilization of languages and a lively visual imagination translated into words.

One of the most memorable services in the course of Amatu'l-Bahá's many travels was the time she spent and the attention she gave to perfectly ordinary people in the peripheries of society. Rúḥíyyih Khánum was at her happiest with villagers, wherever they might have been. When asked what was her favourite spot, the place she had enjoyed most in all her travels, she would often say that it was in the villages and jungles of the world.

She rarely missed the opportunity to validate people in far flung and remote places whom few had heard of and whose simple actions none might ever know. I remember, when we were travelling in Africa, we arrived in a small town on the border of Kenya and Uganda and were invited to lunch in the home of an elderly man, a Bahá'í of some years. They told us he used to work as a cook in the city for the Europeans and had now retired. He had set an elegant table for his precious guest in his small, clean and beautiful hut, with a spotless, brilliant white linen tablecloth and matching napkins, and he served us a most delicious rice and curry. Rúḥíyyih Khánum, who herself loved beautiful table settings, was thrilled and made him feel that his home was a palace and his hospitality that of a king. We never forgot that lunch and I don't think our host ever forgot it either.

How often in the course of these 40 years by her side

did I witness shy, unsure, sometimes dejected human beings uplifted by her genuine kindness, her praise and patience. The lowered head would be raised a little, self-assurance would be restored and dignity regained. Her instinct was to approach people with an open, candid heart, simply and unself-consciously. It was to look for positive qualities in people and verbalize these. But though she was the perfect diplomat in some respects, she was also very direct and often said things frankly and outspokenly. At times she may have hurt people's pride. However, I witnessed how many times she regretted it, how much she felt remorse afterwards if she thought she may have been too harsh with anyone. The driving impulse in all her encounters with the Bahá'ís was to stir them to action and rouse them up so that they would teach the Faith. And often, even when she was critical of individuals, her intent was to protect the Cause. If her manner may at times have appeared abrupt, and initially formidable to those who approached her, it was often the result of her own innate shyness, which few people guessed, for she was disconcerted, to the end of her life, by effusiveness and adulation. While she was a stickler for the respect due to the rank she occupied as Hand of the Cause of God and the widow of Shoghi Effendi, she was the last person to stand on ceremony with the friends.

Seldom did Rúḥíyyih Khánum travel, especially on her longer trips, without a pet. Her love for animals was such that she would gladly accept the extra hardship of tending and cleaning her pets for the simple joy of their company. She used to say, "I get strength and vitality from animals." Her most famous and widely-travelled pets are worthy of mention. There was, for example, the agouti, named Usu after his birth place, the island of Usupoto in

Panama. Usu travelled with her through all the 11 countries in South America, arrived safely in Haifa, and lived a very happy and pampered life for 20 full years. Or there was Tooti, her African Grey parrot from Ghana, who journeyed with us through 30 countries in Africa and gave us a great deal of joy. Tooti was a terrific talker, and learned many languages from the numerous hotel employees along the way; she also announced our arrival everywhere with a loud “Rabbani African Safari”! Or there were the two mischievous chipmunks, Tillie and Chips, and the lame parrot called Horatio who were her companions on her trip to the islands in the Indian Ocean. Or the beautiful baby ocelot she bought from a vendor in a small town in Ecuador, who successfully travelled with us through 13 islands in the West Indies. And of course there were many others. Her motto was, “You only live once; why not get clean joy out of it?”

Rúḥíyyih Khánum was one of the most hard-working human beings that I have ever met. She often used to say, as she kneeled to scrub the tiles or polish the floor or stood on the top of a ladder painting walls and ceilings, “Rúḥíyyih Khánum has done a great many things in life which Mary Maxwell would never have dreamed of doing.” And she never asked anyone to do anything which she had not or could not also have done herself. Much of her hard work was centred on her home in Haifa, which was the hub of continuous activity until the last two and a half years of her life. She kept a regular entourage around her as busy as herself and trained them rigorously in the arts of practical maintenance at the World Centre.

Her first and foremost concern was always the upkeep and care of the Shrines. I remember the only nightmares she ever had, which were very rare, were about some harm done to the Bahá’í Holy Places or disrespect shown towards the Shrines. From the time of the election of the first Universal House of Justice, she assumed the task of educating those of us who were new in Haifa in how to care for the Holy Places. She taught us how to clean the Sacred Shrines, how to wash each crystal in their chandeliers, how to arrange and freshen the flowers, to restore the curtains and curtain linings, how to cover the Thresholds with petals, simply and informally, without rigidity. Her constant reminder was to keep these precious Holy Shrines exactly the way Shoghi Effendi had arranged them. "This is not a place of innovation, but preservation" was her advice to all, and she was acutely sensitive if anyone tried to introduce his or her own likes or dislikes into this area of service. She also undertook periodically to inspect and keep all the Holy Places in order, framing pictures, replacing the frayed and worn out fabrics, keeping an eagle eye on any deviation from the Guardian's ways. When she travelled to countries where she could find fine textiles, table cloths or ornaments needed in the future for these Holy Places or the Shrines, she would purchase these and keep them in the depot, in her home, for future use. For she was a very practical person. She knew these material things would break, grow old, be lost and need to be replaced and she literally created a bank of appropriate furnishings for these Holy Places for the future which were in keeping with the style and taste of the past.

Economy was her constant cry and she deplored waste in any form. How many houses she furnished with second-hand furniture found in her forays in the flea markets of Haifa and Jaffa. How much she saved the Fund with her shrewd bargains and strict economies. The renovation and furnishing of the House of 'Abdu'lláh Páshá engrossed her interest for several years. She collaborated with and helped the Universal House of Justice not

On the roof of the Shrine of the Báb, Rúḥíyyih Khánum examining the tiles for possible repair, 1977

Amatu'l-Bahá in front of the door of her home in Haifa, 1987

Amatu'l-Bahá Rúḥíyyih <u>Kh</u>ánum at the banquet table in the Seat of the Universal House of Justice on the occasion of the 50th anniversary of her marriage to the beloved Guardian, March 24th, 1987; Dr. David Ruhe is presenting the gift of the House of Justice

In her office in Haifa, giving a one-hour, live trans-oceanic telephone interview over station KIEV in California, U.S.A., 1993

only in its renovation, but also in its interior decoration. She searched for and found period Turkish furniture in 'Akká, Nablus and other areas, with the help of Salah Jarrah, the faithful servant of Shoghi Effendi. This House in particular is a masterpiece of her creativity and artistic ability.

One of her most endearing projects in between journeys, when she returned to Haifa, was the never-to-be-forgotten bazaars she organized in her own home. She was consummately skilled at bringing people together and making them work in joy and harmony for a cause. In the case of her wonderful bazaars, this particular cause combined two absorbing interests: the Fund and flea markets. When there were still relatively few of us in Haifa, she would involve almost everyone in helping her, and raised large amounts of money for causes close to her heart, such as the Bahá'í Temple in India, or special teaching projects in different parts of the world. This was one of the many ways in which she brought joy to the House of the Master, which had in the past seen so much grief and sorrow. Without ever violating its sacredness or intruding into its heart of sanctity, she opened wide its doors and filled its rooms with delighted laughter, for she was one of those rare human beings who know how to combine deep reverence and respect with complete freedom of heart and spontaneity of expression.

Another of Amatu'l-Bahá's important social activities in Haifa was her role as the Hostess. Her beautiful library, which was her official dining room for special guests and occasions, and her charming drawing room, which she referred to as "Montreal in Haifa", were the scenes of many elegant dinners and luncheon parties. She loved setting a beautiful table, arranging flowers and overseeing every detail of the event. Apart from formal dinners, she would also give many informal parties, just for fun. After returning from India, every now and then she would be so homesick for that country that she would throw an "Indian Night" party. She would dress the few ladies working at that time in Haifa in her beautiful saris, trace the floors with exquisite patterns made of coloured flour, play Indian music, and we would all enjoy delicious, spicy Indian food under her hospitable roof. And also do the cleaning up with her afterwards! Or there were her exciting "African Nights" when all the friends who were either African or connected to the work in Africa were invited to her home, usually outside in her beautiful garden, and after a scrumptious dinner would drum and sing to their hearts' content. How exhilarating were her dinner parties for the new Counsellors, too, where the guests, numbering over 90 at times, were squeezed into the main hall, as she would say, "with a shoe horn". Even the dignified member of the Universal House of Justice, Charles Wolcott, a distinguished musician himself, was so taken by the spirit of happiness on one of these occasions that he spontaneously played on her large African drum, to the intense joy of Rúḥíyyih Khánum and the African Counsellors. Many hundreds of the friends who met Amatu'l-Bahá on her travels, enjoyed her delightful hospitality and loving attention when visiting Haifa.

There were, of course, a stream of regular nine-day pilgrims with whom she also met, twice a month for nine months of the year, during the course of her last decades in residence in Haifa. This was a custom and responsibility which went back to her earliest years at the side of Shoghi Effendi, and which she dutifully maintained until the last years of her life. She spoke with about 2000 pilgrims each year in the main hall of the Master's House, giving talks which provided guidance and inspiration for many, and she also kept up a voluminous correspondence, encouraging institutions as well as individuals and responding to questions and requests throughout these years.

A particularly important event that took place in Haifa during this period, and one which brought many hundreds of pilgrims flocking through the doors of the Master's House, was the Centenary of the arrival of Bahá'u'lláh in the Holy Land in 1968. That year, two thousand Bahá'ís gathered in Haifa and 'Akká, many of whom had crossed the Mediterranean Sea after attending the Palermo Conference in Sicily. Another extraordinary event in which Rúḥíyyih Khánum participated was the commemoration of the Centenary of the passing of Bahá'u'lláh, during the Holy Year, 1992. On this occasion, three thousand Bahá'ís came to the Holy Land and gathered during the afternoon of May 28th at Bahjí to witness the ceremony during which Amatu'l-Bahá lowered the cylinder containing the Roll of Honour of the Knights of Bahá'u'lláh and placed it in its permanent place at the entrance of the Most Holy Shrine. On the night of His Ascension, after a devotional program in the Ḥaram-i-Aqdas, we all circumambulated that blessed Shrine, the paths round which were lined and lighted by thousands of candles. Rúḥíyyih Khánum spent that night and the night before in the Mansion of Bahjí. She hardly slept the first night for, despite her advanced age by this time, she and her small band of helpers worked until the early hours of the morning carpeting the Shrine with thousands of rose buds and carnations, just as she had done almost 30 years before. When she completed the circumambulation, she went into the Mansion, stood on the balcony and watched in ecstasy and awe the complete ring of Bahá'ís circling round that Holy of Holies.

Amatu'l-Bahá's legacy to us, apart from the rich

memories of her personality and the varied activities associated with her services, also lies in the treasure trove of books she wrote and films she produced. When one contemplates the fullness of her days and years, many of which were spent in travel, one is filled with wonder at how she managed to do so much writing, which involves staying still and without any distractions for long periods of time. When did she ever have sufficient time to write such invaluable books as *The Priceless Pearl*, for example? Often, when asked how she could conduct such a full social life, fulfil so many teaching and administrative obligations and complete such a weighty textbook in the history of our Cause too, she would say, "I worked according to the pattern of Shoghi Effendi when writing *God Passes By*." She gathered and read all her material and facts in one year, making copious notes. Then the following year she wrote the book. Many of her books were written in the pauses between trips. Her *Manual for Pioneers*, written with the practical desire to help many young and inexperienced Bahá'ís across the world, was the result of her observations while travelling in Africa. She began taking notes during her trip and then wrote the book in Haifa after she returned. *The Desire of the World* is a compilation of prayers and personal meditations which she had collected over the years during the dawn hours of the Fast period. *The Ministry of the Custodians*, her masterly compilation covering the interim period before the election of the Supreme Body, includes a powerful introduction written by Amatu'l-Bahá and fills a vital gap in Bahá'í history, covering almost six years of invaluable service of the standard-bearers of the Cause of Bahá'u'lláh. Her last literary work, *Poems of the Passing*, an outpouring of her broken heart after the death of Shoghi Effendi, was printed in 1996 and seems, after her own recent passing,

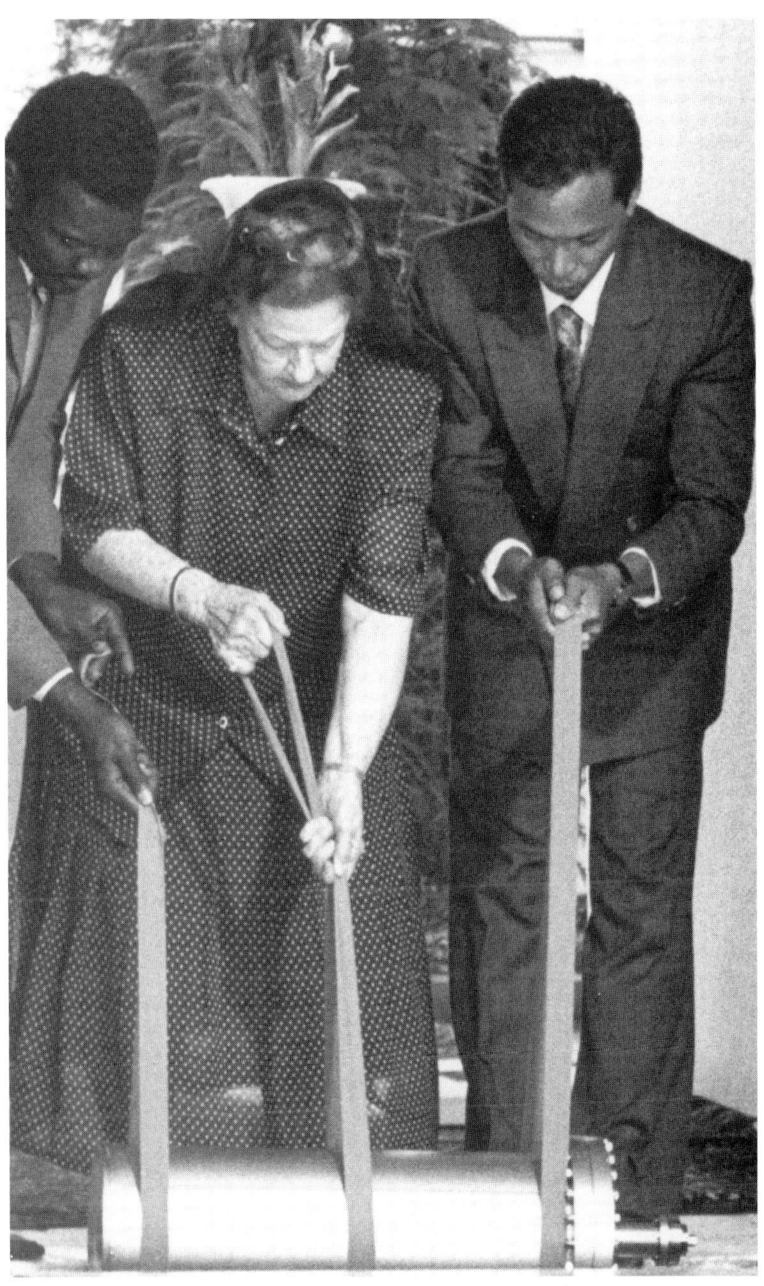

Amatu'l-Bahá Rúḥíyyih Khánum, with helpers, lowering the cylinder in which the Roll of Honour of the Knights of Bahá'u'lláh was placed at the entrance of the Most Holy Shrine, May 28th, 1992

Her joyous and triumphant speech at the second Bahá'í World Congress, New York City, 1992

At the banquet given by Amatu'l-Bahá Rúḥíyyih Khánum in 'Abdu'l-Bahá's home on the occasion of the Counsellors' Conference, December 31st, 1995; she is holding a pair of African drums which were played during that joyous evening

Amatu'l-Bahá at Landegg Academy in Switzerland, giving a talk on her beloved mother, May Maxwell, September 1997

to give us words with which to grieve in turn. Although she had excellent help for typing and other technical matters, Rúḥíyyih Khánum was especially involved with the appearance and layout of all her books, particularly the covers and dust jackets, which she herself always chose and sometimes designed. For some of her publications she even selected the page formatting, and the style and size of the fonts used. She was not content with delegating any tasks which she could do herself and mastered many skills as the result, to oversee their being properly done.

Two documentary films were also produced by Rúḥíyyih Khánum in the course of her life, which she not only featured in herself, but also directed. Even the smallest detail of the editing and sound track in these films were subject to her taste and judgement, for she never engaged in any project if not whole-heartedly. "The Green Light Expedition" was the fruit of her six months' journey in 1975 through the Amazon Basin, the Peruvian and Bolivian altiplano, all the way to the Bush Negroes of Suriname. This two-hour documentary is truly a classic masterpiece, an expression of her concern for the moral as well as the environmental plight of people and places so long ignored and unjustly treated. Her second film, a deeply spiritual experience, is called "The Pilgrimage", and offers a visual pilgrimage to the Holy Shrines and sites of the Bahá'í Holy Places in Haifa and 'Akká, with the privilege of Amatu'l-Bahá as one's guide.

Even if there were all the images of her memorable travels and all the tapes of her talks at our disposal, how is it possible to encompass a life as rich and broad as that of Amatu'l-Bahá Rúḥíyyih Khánum's in this inadequate frame of words? She touched and filled my life and the lives of numerous people everywhere around the world, not only by giving us a desire to serve but also by bringing us joy and laughter, and her relationships have linked many people over the years. But the primary source of comfort and happiness to Amatu'l-Bahá herself in the last decades of her life was, above all else, her love for the Universal House of Justice and her bond with this Institution and its individual members. Every single year, from the time of its inception in 1963, on the anniversary of the passing of the beloved Guardian, she received most heart-warming, most loving tributes from the Supreme Body to the victories she had won in the previous year. Each Naw-Rúz too, or on the occasion of her return from her long travels, and also on her birthday, she received loving and encouraging personal messages from the Universal House of Justice which warmed her heart. In March of 1987, on the 50th anniversary of her marriage to the beloved Guardian, the Universal House of Justice gave a banquet in her honour in the majestic banquet hall of its Seat. This honour was repeated a decade later on the anniversary of her 60th year in the Holy Land, and it meant more to her than could be expressed in words. When all nine members of the Universal House of Justice came to her home for the last time three weeks before her passing and paid their respects, when she was quite frail and in bed, such a deep sense of happiness and contentment enveloped her that it was tangible, like sunlight, in the room after they left. She lingered quietly in that light a moment, and then said—"I felt their love; they are my closest friends." This bond, which symbolized her total dedication to the Covenant throughout her life, was strong and vibrant to the end and always reciprocal.

About two weeks before her passing, she was in her bed with her eyes closed. I thought she was asleep, when suddenly she opened her eyes, turned towards me and said, "Remember, white over black". She repeated this twice, and again closed her eyes. I did not know if she had been dreaming or thinking about something specific. When she passed away, I remembered this, and remembered too the square piece of black silk velvet which she owned that was lined and embroidered so beautifully with exquisite gold thread. She had used this a few times for the funerals of very special people, such as the Hands of the Cause Milly Collins and Ṭarázu'lláh Samandarí, as well as Ethel Revell. We covered her casket with this, and placed along its full length a most delicate floral arrangement of white rose buds, fuchsias and tubular roses. Was this what she had seen?

How befitting her funeral was, held in the large central hall of the Master's House where she had chaired the election of the first Universal House of Justice. Accordingly, we followed the same pattern that she had set on that significant occasion and removed the doors to the four sides of the hall in order to arrange seats for the large number of people attending her funeral service. The two Hands of the Cause were present, together with members of the Universal House of Justice, the International Teaching Centre Counsellors, and twenty-four Continental Counsellors from all over the world. Also attending were her family members and representatives from 76 National Spiritual Assemblies, senior officials from the Canadian and United States embassies, representatives of the Israeli government, the mayors of Haifa and 'Akká, other prominent Israeli citizens and a number of special invited guests. The hall and both sides of the front entrance were filled with beautiful floral arrangements which overflowed down the steps and into the garden of her home. Following the readings and the chanting of the Prayer for the Dead, she left for the last time that house which she had entered as a bride 63 years before, her coffin carried by members of the Universal House of Justice. This beautifully crafted coffin of clear American cedar was borne across the street and lowered into its vault in the centre of the garden opposite by believers representing a variety of ethnic origins. Her resting-place, too, was heaped on each side by a tribute of flowers from those who loved her all over the planet, though despite their volume, how few they seemed before her great achievements. Almost 1,000 people, including pilgrims and volunteers serving at the Bahá'í World Centre, stood outside her home and in the closed-off street, as well as in the garden where her grave had been prepared. The interior of the grave was carpeted on all sides with hundreds of roses and carnations, just as she had arranged for her beloved Shoghi Effendi 42 years before. And as the rain poured down, more prayers were recited and chanted before her casket was lowered into the ground. The rainstorm which had begun on the night she passed away finally subsided to a drizzle as her precious remains were laid to rest, and it seemed to me then as though the skies were mingling their tears with those of all who loved, admired and cherished her.

I think, to sum up such a life, there are no adequate words but those expressed in the message of the Universal House of Justice to the Bahá'í world after her passing:

19 January 2000

To the Bahá'ís of the World

In the early hours of this morning, the soul of Amatu'l-Bahá Rúḥíyyih Khánum, beloved consort of Shoghi Effendi and the Bahá'í world's last remaining link with the family of 'Abdu'l-Bahá, was released from the limitations of this earthly existence. In the midst of our grief, we are sustained by our confidence that she has been gathered to the glory of the Concourse on High in the presence of the Abhá Beauty.

For all whose hearts she touched so deeply, the sorrow that this irreparable loss brings will, in God's good time, be assuaged in awareness of the joy that is hers through her reunion with the Guardian and with the Master, Who had Himself prayed in the Most Holy Shrine that her parents be blessed with a child. Down the centuries to come, the followers of Bahá'u'lláh will contemplate with wonder and gratitude the quality of the services—ardent, indomitable, resourceful—that she brought to the protection and promotion of the Cause.

In her youth, Amatu'l-Bahá had already distinguished herself through her activities in North America, and later, both with her dear mother and on her own, she had rendered valuable service to the Cause in Europe. Her twenty years of intimate association with Shoghi Effendi evoked from his pen such accolades as "my helpmate", "my shield", "my tireless collaborator in the arduous tasks I shoulder." To these tributes he added in 1952 his decision to elevate her to the rank of Hand of the Cause of God, after the death of her illustrious father.

The devastating shock of the beloved Guardian's passing steeled her resolve to lend her share, with the other Hands of the Cause, to the triumph of the Ten Year Crusade, and subsequently to undertake, with characteristic intrepidity, her historic worldwide travels.

A life so noble in its provenance, so crucial to the

preservation of the Faith's integrity, and so rich in its dedicated, uninterrupted and selfless service, moves us to call for befitting commemorations by Bahá'í communities on both national and local levels, as well as for special gatherings in her memory in all Houses of Worship.

With yearning hearts, we supplicate at the Holy Threshold for infinite heavenly bounties to surround her soul, as she assumes her rightful and well-earned position among the exalted company in the Abhá Kingdom.

The Universal House of Justice

Her last pubiic talk – Amatu'l-Bahá opening the Eighth International Bahá'í Convention in Haifa, 1998

The three Hands of the Cause of God at the International Teaching Centre in Haifa, 1998. Left to right: ‘Alí Akbar Furútan, Amatu’l-Bahá Rúḥíyyih <u>Kh</u>ánum and ‘Alí-Muḥammad Varqá

THE FUNERAL
The casket in the main hall of the Master's House during the service,
January 23rd, 2000

Members of the Universal House of Justice carrying the casket from the main hall of the Master's House, January 23rd, 2000

Lowering of the casket, January 23rd, 2000

The interior of the grave was carpeted with fresh flowers

A view of her beautiful and peaceful park, opposite the Master's House, where her precious remains were laid to rest

IV

Highlights of Her Travels

O that I could travel, even though on foot and in the utmost poverty, to these regions, and, raising the call of "Yá Bahá'u'l-Abhá" in cities, villages, mountains, deserts and oceans, promote the divine teachings! This, alas, I cannot do. How intensely I deplore it! Please God, ye may achieve it.

'Abdu'l-Bahá

RIDING BAREBACK IN A SARI

Amatu'l-Bahá sits behind a mahout on a work elephant in the jungles of Mysore, 1964

In the village of Jarkorachi, Bolivia, 1967, Amatu'l-Bahá Rúḥíyyih Khánum, dressed in her Bolivian outfit, among people she dearly loved

In the village of Los Muchos, Venezuela, 1968, with the Guajiro family of Cecilia Iquarar, one of the distinguished Bahá'ís of the area. Rúḥíyyih <u>Kh</u>ánum is holding Rogero, the son of the family

Amatu'l-Bahá in African dress, with her Land Rover which she drove 36,000 miles through 34 countries on her "Great African Safari", from 1969–1973, photographed in Nairobi, Kenya

At the Youth Conference in Fiesch, Switzerland, 1971.
Amatu'l-Bahá was always very happy when amongst the
Bahá'í youth

Amatu'l-Bahá spent the night in this tent on a freezing cold night in the village of Kungwane, in the Kalahari Desert, in June of 1972

Rúḥíyyih Khánum was dressed in full formal Swazi costume and was asked to dance with the young girls at the "Reed Dance" Festival before the King, 1972

Amatu'l-Bahá in Kodiak, Alaska, 1973

Amatu'l-Bahá Rúḥíyyih Khánum in Point Barrow, the most northerly point of Alaska, the Arctic Sea in the background, August 1973

With her crew on "The Green Light Expedition", 1975. Prayers were said on the roof of this boat.

Amatu'l-Bahá helping to free their boat from a sand bar. "The Green Light Expedition", 1975

Amatu'l-Bahá Rúḥíyyih Khánum laying the cornerstone of the Bahá'í Temple in Delhi, India, helped by the architect, Fariburz Sahba, 1977

Outside the door of the meeting house, with its beautiful traditional carvings, of the Orakei Marae in Auckland, New Zealand, 1979

Amatu'l-Bahá in Panama, 1981

Amatu'l-Bahá with the Gordon children, in Alberta, Canada, 1982

Rúḥíyyih <u>Kh</u>ánum flanked by two Elders in a village in Papua New Guinea, 1984

Amatu'l-Bahá sitting on the bow of her 7-metre-long dugout canoe. She visited the villages of the Gulf Province in Papua New Guinea, 1984

On the day of the dedication of the Mother Temple of India,
1986

Amatu'l-Bahá Rúḥíyyih <u>Kh</u>ánum with some of the Bahá'ís of Greenland at the "Spirit North" Conference held in Frobisher Bay, Baffin Island, Northwest Territories, Canada, 1986

Rúḥíyyih <u>Kh</u>ánum's arrival in Calgary, Alberta, Canada, 1986

Amatu'l-Bahá at the inauguration of the Maxwell International Bahá'í School, Canada, 1989

Amatu'l-Bahá Rúḥíyyih Khánum with the Lt. Governor of British Columbia, 1989, at the formal inauguration of the Maxwell International Bahá'í School

Rúḥíyyih <u>Kh</u>ánum in Macau, 1989, at the dedication of the new premises of the Bahá'í School, "School of the Nations"

Amatu'l-Bahá was met at the border of Kyrgyzstan by the Minister of Religion, Mr. Aziz, and escorted by him to her hotel in Bishkek, 1993

Arrival in Ulan Bator, Mongolia for the first National Convention,
flanked by two very active believers, 1994

Amatu'l-Bahá receiving a gift from His Holiness Catholicos-Patriarch of All Georgia Iliya II at the Patriarchate in Tblisi, Georgia, 1995

Planting a memorial tree in Iguaçu at the famous Haipa
Power Plant in Foz do Iguaçu, Brazil, 1996

HER 87TH BIRTHDAY

Celebrated in the National Hazíratu'l-Quds in Madrid, Spain – 8 August 1997